WONDERHELL

WHY SUCCESS DOESN'T FEEL LIKE IT SHOULD...
AND WHAT TO DO ABOUT IT

to set your intentions and priorities, learn to find peace, and embrace the potential for the life you've always wanted—read this book!"

—**DR. MARSHALL GOLDSMITH**, Thinkers50 #1 Executive Coach, *New York Times* best-selling author of *What Got You Here Won't Get You There*

"Laura Gassner Otting reimagines the stories we tell ourselves about success and shows how mixed emotions like fear, uncertainty, and stress that accompany success are often a sign that we're on the right track."

—**OZAN VAROL**, Best-selling author of *Think Like a Rocket Scientist*

"If you want to feel seen, heard, and affirmed for who you are and who you are becoming—Wonderhell is the must-have guide for a journey that can often feel lonely."

—**MINDA HARTS**, Best-selling author of *The Memo*

"With actionable insights and an intuitive framework, *Wonderhell* is a bold invitation that every entrepreneur must read."

—**KARA GOLDIN**, Founder of Hint Water, *Wall Street Journal* best-selling author of *Undaunted*

"A wise, loving, laugh-out-loud funny guide / kick in the pants for navigating the inevitable (but rarely discussed) fear we face on the path to success. For anyone who wants to be more and do more, *Wonderhell* will help you turn confusion into confidence, exhaustion into exhilaration, and worry into winning."

—**DR. TASHA EURICH**, Organizational Psychologist, *New York Times* best-selling author of *Bankable Leadership* and *Insight*

"*Wonderhell* is an essential book for those who are ready to push themselves to new heights. Full of inspiring stories of people who dared to ask more of themselves, Laura offers research, tips, and tools in an easy, fast read so that you can push forward with confidence through the messy middle."

—**ERICA DHAWAN**, Author of *Digital Body Language*

"Laura's decades of experience as an executive recruiter shine in *Wonderhell*. She offers readers practical and powerful tools to achieve consistent success that's delivered with her trademark warmth and wit. If you're on the dangerous and exciting cusp of becoming more than you thought you could be—or you dream of getting there—then Laura Gassner Otting's new book is for you."

—**DORIE CLARK**, *Wall Street Journal* best-selling author of *The Long Game*, executive education faculty, Duke University Fuqua School of Business

"I count myself lucky that Laura Gassner Otting responds to my texts. Sure, I'll brag that I have that kind of unbridled access to someone who has both had success and knows how to help others achieve it. Thankfully, her brainy new book, *Wonderhell*, is much more than a few text messages. Now, you too can benefit from her unique perspectives, powerful thoughts, and actionable strategies to better manage your present and future opportunities. When doubt creeps (or when the ego wails 'You deserve this!'), *Wonderhell* is here to provide balance and a healthier approach to keep things going in the right direction. What a ride!"

—**MITCH JOEL**, Founder of ThinkersOne, host of *Six Pixels of Separation*

"If you've ever gone further and achieved more than you thought you could ... and then gone, 'Now what?!' ... this is the book for you. *Wonderhell* shows you not only how to make the most of your present success, but what it takes to go further still."

—**MICHAEL BUNGAY STANIER**, Author of *The Coaching Habit* and *How to Begin*

"You will realize you are not alone after reading these incredible stories of triumph and tragedy from so many different people and perspectives. *Wonderhell* is a masterclass filled with humor, truth, and a bit of edge. If you feel lost, if you feel alone, if you feel stuck ... this book is for you."

—**TIFFANI BOVA**, *Wall Street Journal* best-selling author of *Growth IQ*

"LGO's unique take on a seriously under-discussed success truth is both illuminating and incredibly timely. Her practical guidance is truly invaluable for today's high performers—especially those looking to invest their time and energy with more intentionality and clarity."

—**ERIN KING**, Author of *You're Kind of a Big Deal*

"*Wonderhell* takes a deep dive into the gap between who you were and who you've become so you can experience your full potential without limit (and help others do the same), now! Laura Gassner Otting inspires me again and again!"

—**RICHIE NORTON**, Award-winning author of *Anti-Time Management* and *The Power of Starting Something Stupid*

WONDERHELL

Why Success Doesn't Feel Like It Should . . .
and What to Do About It

LAURA GASSNER OTTING

IDEAPRESS
PUBLISHING

WASHINGTON, DC

IDEAPRESS
PUBLISHING

Paperback Edition

Ideapress Publishing | www.ideapresspublishing.com

All trademarks are the property of their respective companies.

Cover Design: Zoe Norvell
Interior Design: I Need a Book Interior
Illustrations: Jessica Angerstein, Lillian Chase, and Jonathan Rambinintsoa

Cataloging-in-Publication Data is on file with the Library of Congress.

Hardcover ISBN: 978-1-64687-122-3
Paperback ISBN: 978-1-64687-171-1

Special Sales

Ideapress Books are available at a special discount for bulk purchases for sales promotions and premiums, or for use in corporate training programs. Special editions, including personalized covers, a custom foreword, corporate imprints, and bonus content, are also available.

1 2 3 4 5 6 7 8 9 10

To Jonathan, Benjamin, and Tobias,
who are the wonder in any hell.

Contents

The gods have two ways of dealing harshly with us.
The first is to deny us our dreams,
and the second is to grant them.

—Oscar Wilde

THE INFORMATION DESK

WELCOME TO
WONDERHELL

Preface

★

It's working!

That thing you created, you built, you launched—it's working. You weren't so sure you could pull it off, but you did. And it feels exciting, incredible, amazing.

Success! It's wonderful, right? The work you did opened more doors than you *ever* thought possible. But that work also teased the opportunity of even more doors that you'd *never* thought possible.

And maybe, just maybe, as you peeked through those new doors into what could be . . . you admitted something to yourself.

I want more.

In this transformative moment, everything changes. There was the *you* before this moment, and then there is the *you* after it. And now you can't go back.

Instead of success bringing you happiness, it handed you an increased hunger, a faster pace, and bigger goals. And within that increased hunger, that faster pace, and those bigger goals, you also found uncertainty, self-doubt, anxiety, and stress.

Success is *wonderful*. But it's also *hell*.

Success is *Wonderhell*.

Wonderhell is the self-taught sales rep who wasn't sure she could close even one deal and now is striving to reach the platinum-level corporate award she thought was reserved only for others.

It's the eager entrepreneur who started his own business only to realize that its explosive growth demands an understanding of infrastructure and operations that he doesn't yet possess.

It's the high-level executive who stood in for her boss at an event and discovered she loves the challenges of being center stage.

Wonderhell is you, in the space between your past success and your next accomplishment—between who you were and who you just realized you can become.

In a way, success is like an amusement park. You looked forward to it for a long time, and when you finally got there, everything seemed great at first. You were starting to have fun. But as the day wears on, with the heat of the sun blazing and the corndogs and cotton candy churning in your belly ride after ride, you begin to have doubts.

I'm not sure I want to be here.

This was supposed to be fun.

Wait, this actually kind of sucks.

We expect success to be an enjoyable ride, but it's more like a terrifying gauntlet of never-ending challenges. Why isn't everything easier? Why doesn't success feel better? Why does it feel like Wonderhell?

You've picked up this book because you have a dream, a plan, a demon, a potential, an unshakable goal that excites you and scares you at the same time. Maybe you think that goal is silly or even impossible, but it's not. You are simply in Wonderhell.

I have been there, too, and needed to find a way through it. So I sought out answers from more than one hundred others who made it to the other side. This book tells some of their stories. You can read it from cover to cover, or hop around from section to section, just as you would move through the rides at that amusement park, depending on your own needs and desires.

Yes, I know. That approach is unique. But so are you. So is your journey. And so is your Wonderhell, full of your very own aspirations, burdens, flops, and achievements.

We have come to see this space of uncertainty, doubt, and overwhelm as the *breakdown*, but what if it is really a *breakthrough*?

What if instead of bracing to survive in this liminal space, this middle of the middle, we learn to thrive in it instead?

What if success isn't an endpoint, but a portal to all that you can become?

What if the path to your next great success is on the other side?

Are you ready for your Wonderhell?

Let's find out.

Introduction

★

It was 4:28 a.m. Or maybe it was 7:28 a.m. It might even have been 1:28 a.m.

Over the prior three weeks, I'd gone to sleep in ten different time zones and woken up in twenty new hotel beds. But at this moment, I was somewhere around 35,000 feet in the air with 1,200 miles behind me and 1,200 more to go. I knew only one thing for certain: somewhere between the blur that was the past and the blur that would be the future was the space I was in at present: upright and locked in a center seat on a red-eye flight, headed home at last—completely and utterly fried.

A couple of years earlier, I had given the very first big, public speech of my life, all the while hoping my stomach wouldn't make a break for the exit. That speech launched a career change I never knew I could have and prompted me to write a book I never knew I could write. Now, as I was finishing the launch campaign for that book, I wondered if anyone would even read it.

I was nine toes over the edge of incompetence, teetering precariously with no safety net in sight.

The book's launch demanded that I be bold. So I had wrestled all of my impostor-syndrome demons to the ground, hushed every inner voice forbidding me to ask for help, and kicked the shins of my well-mannered instincts, which wanted me to pipe down and not make a fuss. I had no idea what I was doing, but I set crazy goals for myself anyway.

I let my mouth write a whole lot of checks that my hustle had to cash.

But it worked, and the book became a best seller.

Destination reached!

Success achieved!

I was honored. I was humbled. I was overwhelmed. And sitting on that red-eye flight, I was also bone-tired.

The exhaustion at that moment was unlike anything I'd felt before. Sure, I'd been tired after having two babies. But that was a marathon type of slog, where I just had to quiet the raging hormones on their quest for rebalance as they screamed in my sleep-deprived inner ear, *You have no idea what you're doing!* (Twenty years later, I can tell you their prediction wasn't exactly wrong.) And I'd been tired with, you know, *actual* marathons that I decided to run as misfired midlife crises—26.2-mile battles against every part of me, as my body and mind telegraphed that the torture was wholly untenable.

This exhaustion was different.

I had spent the better part of the launch campaign existing on nothing but coffee, protein bars, and the rush of adrenaline that bowel-shaking terror always provides. I'd like to say that along the way I'd found my rhythm, my flow, my stride, but that would be untrue. By the end of the campaign, I was still just as much of a moxie-filled bag of curious awkwardness as ever. But this thing I created, I grew, I birthed, I pursued so very hard for those weeks and months and years: it was working.

And squeezed into the middle seat on that airplane, suspended halfway between origin and destination, I heard a tiny voice from within. Rising from somewhere in the alchemy of achievement and exhaustion, bubbling up past the part of my brain that normally governs my humility, it whispered insistently: *This thing has legs . . . This thing has legs!*

This murmur of grandeur set my altitude-addled mind on a mission to choreograph the gymnastics it might take to reach a new level of success—one that I'd never imagined was open to me before.

Wait! I thought. *Maybe I haven't reached my destination at all. Maybe I can go even farther.*

That idea was mind-blowing. It was electrifying. It was wonderful.

But it was also anxiety-provoking. It was stress-inducing. It was hell.

It was wonderful. And it was hell.

I was no longer just jammed into that too-small seat on that too-long flight. I was somewhere else entirely.

I was in Wonderhell.

And en route to Wonderhell, I had packed more than my fancy new bestseller bio. Crammed into my carry-on suitcase was something else, too, something that would forever change me: an expanded vision of my potential.

This was not the first time I felt stressed in a high-pressure situation or wondered whether I was setting my goals at the right level. But it was the first time I had consciously experienced such a fundamental shift in my understanding of who I *could* be. It was the most sudden expansion in my expectations for myself—an entirely new perception of my capabilities in relation to my success. It was the earliest crystallization in my mind of that intersection between the wonder of newly available opportunities and the hell of my potential.

Yes, I was squarely in Wonderhell.

And all I could ask myself was: *How on earth do I get out of here?!*

Success Is Not the Final Destination

I bet you've been in Wonderhell, too. If you're anything like me—yes, I see you!—you've had this moment of realization, when you're standing on a current success while reaching toward the next one. And if you're anything like me, you recognize this as the moment when the burden of your potential slinks into your psyche, unpacks its tent, and camps the hell out.

Are you going to live into this opportunity? it asks. *Or are you going to let it pass on by, risking a future of haunting regret?*

The burden of your potential attaches itself to your shoulders and demands that you carry it around in your backpack and serve it at all times. Oh yes, your ego has entered the chat. And it starts to hum the moment you recognize that your idea has promise, your dream can be bigger, you were meant for more. You can have everything you've ever wanted—if only you agree to your potential's ever-increasing demands.

We think about success as if it is a final destination—as if it means that we've arrived, that we are at our journey's conclusion. *Smooth sailing*, we tell ourselves. *Easy money*. But it's not.

Wonderhell teaches us that each success is not a final destination at all, but an inflection point on that lifelong journey.

A Way through Wonderhell

In the months and years since this red-eye realization, I've continued to travel around the world promoting my book and engaging with diverse audiences of all ages, in all stages of life. I've heard time and again the tales of innovators, entrepreneurs, instigators, and iconoclasts who found themselves smack in the middle of their own personal Wonderhell—though most of them didn't recognize it at the time. Some thrived in it. Some drowned in it. And I couldn't get it out of my head. In their stories, there are lessons for all of us.

When the COVID-19 pandemic hit, I used the lockdown as an opportunity to study the topic of not just *surviving* one's experience with success, but *thriving* in it. I attempted to crush it, to lean in, to adopt a 10x mindset—and for what it's worth, I also tried to wash my face, stop apologizing, and become a #girlboss. If it was a best-selling self-help tome, I tried it. And failed.

Social media was not helpful either. There, it seemed that success came in only two forms: the hustleporn, slicked-back, suited-up bros jetting off to ink their next deal, or the boho-chic instafluencers imploring me to follow my passion and promising me happiness if only I could breathe into the right energy crystals. (What even are energy crystals, anyway?)

None of this worked for me. And it might not work for you either. It certainly didn't work for the thousands of leaders whom I steered through pivotal career and life shifts during my twenty-year career in executive search. And it certainly didn't work for the nearly one hundred glass-ceiling breakers, Olympic medalists, start-up unicorns, and everyday people—like you and like me—whom I interviewed in search of a way through Wonderhell.

Each one of these successful individuals talked about doing what they never thought possible. And each one of them also shared how, at each stage and at each phase, they experienced a crushing combination of doubt, vulnerability, envy, impostor syndrome, exhaustion, and burnout. But each one made it to the other side of Wonderhell—and was the better for it.

So, how did they do it? More important, could any one of us learn to do the same?

Three main pathways emerged, pointing the way through Wonderhell.

Embracing the Burden of Your Potential

First, they came to terms with their ambition, realizing that their original idea of success was merely a pit stop en route to something even bigger.

You see, success isn't the final destination at all, but a portal—a door that opens to reveal your truest self and purpose—an invitation to achieve and become more than you ever thought possible.

I saw this phenomenon firsthand as an executive recruiter assisting organizations large and small in the search for C-suite talent, interviewing thousands of leaders at these trajectory-defining moments of professional transition. From time to time, we would have an internal candidate—someone currently employed in the organization but in a lower-level role. And every single time, internal candidates who didn't get the bigger job eventually left. Why? Because the very process of interviewing for it meant that, just for a moment, they had to wear the clothes of that role, speak in the voice of that role, and imagine the scenarios of life in that role. And once they did, they couldn't unsee themselves in that bigger role.

Just like those internal candidates, you cannot unsee this new you.

Each time you imagine the next level of success, you see a version of yourself that you never knew existed, a potential that you never thought could be real, a promise of who you could become and what you could embody if only you allowed yourself to play for a while in that uncomfortable, uncertain place.

Coming to terms with your ambition requires you to learn how to play bigger, make your own luck, figure out who you are, live into your truest self, and let go of the demons that have been haunting you. We will walk through these topics in more detail in Impostortown.

Renegotiating Your Relationship with Mixed Emotions

Second, those people I interviewed with a track record of thriving in Wonderhell understood that uncomfortable feelings surrounding success aren't just an obligatory part of the process, but incredibly helpful allies.

In other words, the mixed emotions—the good, the bad, and the ugly—surrounding this discovery of the new you aren't *limitations*, but *invitations*. They are a sign that you're on the right track, navigating toward new opportunities and new growth. And so those who thrived in Wonderhell were able to pause and listen to these emotions, reflect on them, learn from them, and renegotiate their relationship with them.

We are told that these uncomfortable emotions are just a "necessary evil," a byproduct of going after everything we've ever wanted; we just need to hang on by our fingernails and somehow get through the stressful, unwanted side effects of success, trying to survive these difficult moments while torturing ourselves with a never-ending, flip-flopping internal dialogue: *I can handle this. Wait . . . can I handle this?*

But that survival story is a lie, and that lie is holding you back from capitalizing on your Wonderhell.

Wonderhell isn't a necessary evil. It's the excitement and the fear, the joy and the anxiety, the possibility and the uncertainty, the promise and the pressure you feel when you see this potential new you, and when you realize that the only one who gets to choose which *you* to become is . . . well, you.

And this means changing the doomsaying voice inside of your head—the one screaming, "You haven't *done* this before!" and warning you to run from your potential—into a voice cheering, "You haven't done *this* before!" and encouraging you to run toward it.

Renegotiating your relationship with the mixed emotions about success means you'll need to manage uncertainty, fly without a net, find your own way, gain perspective on other people, and prepare to go farther together. We will journey through these checkpoints in Doubtsville.

Doing It Again . . . and Again . . . and Again . . .

Third, for every single person I interviewed, what was on the other side of this Wonderhell was simply the next one, and the next one, and (if they were lucky) the next one after that.

Wonderhell, it seems, loves itself a repeat visitor.

We think that things will settle down after we crush that next goal, that we just need to get through this one stomach-churning, butt-clenching, fight-or-flight moment, as if it's a short-term, one-time hurdle. But in reality, each of our journeys is a series of successes punctuated by losses, by lessons, by life. It's an ongoing cycle. There isn't one big finish line, but a million different little ones.

Look, I'm not telling you to "Suck it up, sis!" I'm not advising you to "Get hard, bro!" What I am saying is this: Accepting your most recent success as a finite destination would mean there is also a finite limit to your growth. And all this does is steal the wonder and leave you in only the hell.

Whether your ambition is spoken out loud with intention, printed in giant letters on your vision board, or just a whispered voice that catches you by surprise, the path to achieving your new, bigger goals runs straight through your personal Wonderhell (again and again and again . . .). Getting comfortable in this repeated, cyclical journey demands that you say no to hustleporn, focus on what really matters, quiet your perfectionistic tendencies, stand tall when the floor drops out, and adopt a beginner's mindset. We will explore these routes at length in Burnout City.

An Invitation to Enjoy the Ride

What if, all along, you've been miscategorizing this space that linked *where you've already been* and *what you've just learned is possible?*

What if everything you have achieved or will become, large or small, is simply a preamble to what you can achieve or become next?

What if, instead of dreading Wonderhell and merely surviving it, you could learn to look forward to it and actually thrive in it instead?

What if Wonderhell isn't just a temporary state of mind, but your new permanent home?

This book is my invitation to you: Join me in Wonderhell! Come learn from those who have been fueled and fed by the ride—those who overcame, slayed, or embraced the hell so they could live freely in the wonder.

Some of them had to quiet their impostor syndrome—to accept that they belong; that they are worthy of their goals; that they can achieve anything and everything they want; and that it's okay to want something so big, they can only whisper it to themselves.

Some had to banish their self-doubt—their self-fulfilling prophecy about success being out of reach or only for someone else, about their goals being too big, too hairy, too audacious.

Some had to adjust to, anticipate, or eradicate the burnout that resulted when their current life was unable to support the weight of the possibility they imagined.

Some learned to fly their freak flag. Some learned to let go. Some chose to grow big, and others decided to stay the course.

The stories of some people in this book will sound so familiar that you could swap your name for theirs, while the stories of others will feel entirely out of your orbit. Yet the lessons you'll learn from the distress, discomfort, and discombobulation that any type of growth demands—these lessons are the same for every single person here. They were all in their own hell, and each of them navigated through it to find their own wonder on the other side.

And you can, too.

Welcome to Wonderhell!

I'm glad you're here.

HAUNTED HOUSE

Letting Go of
Your Demons

TENT OF
ODDITIES

Living into Your
Truest Self

HALL OF
MIRRORS

Figuring Out
Who You Are

THE
FORTUNE
TELLER

Making Your
Own Luck

THE
IMAGINARIUM

Learning to
Play Bigger

IMPOSTORTOWN

YOU
ARE
HERE

IMPOSTORTOWN

EMBRACE YOUR
AMBITION

The gates of Wonderhell are your personal portal to your next big success. Through those gates, you glimpse the tantalizing future you never even knew you wanted or could achieve. Every bit of that future success can be yours, if only you are bold enough to believe in it—and go after it.

So, what's stopping you? Is it that disparaging voice in your head that accuses you of being a fraud? Each time you level up, so does that inner critic, wondering:

Who am I to dare to dream this big?

Will my luck run out at this next level?

What if they figure out that I don't know what I'm doing?

Can I still be successful as the real me?

How do I let go of everyone else's expectations of me?

It's time to stop shrinking into the smaller box built for you by others—or even the safe, secure, but suffocating box you built for yourself—and start taking up a space of your own. It's time to embrace your ambition.

First stop: Impostortown!

Wait, you don't feel like you belong here? Perfect! Neither does anyone else.

Learning to Play Bigger

★

Step right up to the Imaginarium, where dreams and delights appear in a pageant of possibilities! In this gallery of wonders, your true potential will be exposed. The new, more expansive view of yourself nestles within your mind, and it won't be dislodged no matter what you do. You enter the Imaginarium as one person, but you will leave as another person entirely, with bigger, bolder aspirations and an expanded sense of what your life could be.

Every Great Story Starts with Guns N' Roses

Simon Tam wanted to play rock 'n' roll for as long as he could remember. Instead, he found himself at the Supreme Court with his identity at stake.

Like every great story, Simon's started with Guns N' Roses. "I grew up in the eighties watching their music videos and thinking, 'That's what I want to do,'" Simon says. He spent several years floating in and out of makeshift bands until finally, in 2006, he formed the world's first all–Asian American dance rock band, The Slants.

The Slants found huge success, played loads of concerts, and sold out big halls. They were living the dream—traveling from gig to gig with guitars and drums and amps and mics all packed into their rickety van—and as long as the van was running, things were great! That is, until they talked to a lawyer who recommended trademarking their name to protect their intellectual property.

Simon was assured that this would take no more than six months and cost just a few hundred bucks. But then the US Patent and Trademark Office denied the request, claiming that the band's name was racist and offensive.

The band members had brainstormed the name themselves when they mused about what they had in common. "Slanted eyes?" someone joked. Simon thought that was interesting because, first, it's factually incorrect: Asians have eyes of various shapes and aren't the only people whose eyes appear narrow or tapered. But the name worked in another way, too.

"We could talk about our perspective—our 'slant' on life—as people of color navigating the entertainment industry," Simon points out. "At the same time, we could pay homage to the Asian American activists who had been using the term in a reappropriated, self-empowering way." The government disagreed, and the band was left with a choice: compromise part of their identity and find a new name, or fight the decision.

Simon decided to play bigger. Simon chose to fight.

Into the van, along with the guitars and drums and amps and mics, now went legal briefs and law books. The more Simon dug into the issue, the more he learned this law was being enforced in a way that was harming those it was intended to serve, preventing people like him from turning hurtful language and symbols into badges of pride and honor.

As he fought court case after court case, legal bills piled up next to broken-down van bills. It absorbed time and attention. He was forced to take on extra jobs to pay for it. He lost bandmates over it. But Simon recognized an opportunity to make a difference, and he couldn't go back.

In 2017, the Slants won a unanimous, landmark case before the Supreme Court, helping expand civil liberties for marginalized populations. Simon's work has since been featured in 150 different countries and highlighted in over three thousand media outlets, including *Rolling Stone*, *Time*, the *New York Times*, NPR, and the BBC. And Simon and the Slants haven't just rested their case. Leading this fight opened Simon's imagination to an even bigger purpose still: starting The Slants Foundation, a nonprofit that supports arts and activism projects for underrepresented communities. "Supporting the arts is more than just charity or entertainment," he says. "It's justice."

Fewer Pantyhose, Bigger Dreams

When it comes to the stories we commonly hear, whether in the news or in the lives of our neighbors and friends, we tend to be fed the big moments: *This person started this business, ran this marathon, won this case.* Seldom do we learn about the little moments that lead up to those big ones. But often those important moments take place riding down the highway, surrounded by guitars and drums and amps and mics, in the back of a rickety van.

For me, one of those moments happened in a corner office in downtown Boston.

When my executive recruiting company was about five years old, I got the call of most entrepreneurs' dreams. "Laura, we've been watching you," beckoned the voice of opportunity. "We like what you're doing. Would you consider being acquired?"

Someone wanted to buy my business—the business-baby I birthed while birthing two human babies on the side, the business-soul that had shocked me by becoming no small part of my identity. Someone had seen my success and wanted a piece of it for themselves.

It was heady and ego-stroking, a validation that all those sleepless nights of entrepreneurial insomnia (piled on top of maternal insomnia) were worth it. I was counting my money before I even hung up the phone.

We went through the necessary due diligence, strategy sessions, and paperwork—all the usual courtship rigmarole. At last, it was time for the big meeting to consummate the relationship, and what was I thinking?

Show me the money.

That morning, I got all dolled up in my most professional finery: navy blue suit and power pumps. I had even bought pantyhose (*ugh!*) for the occasion. At the department store the previous day—flipping through the hosiery sizes with one hand while wrangling a toddler and a preschooler with the other—I'd tried to decipher that periodic table on the back of the package,

wondering, *Where exactly on this triangular grid does my post-baby booty land?*
But there I was, walking into the building at last—*fapitzed*,[1] as my nana would
pronounce—like a real grown-up business lady. Dare I say, there might even
have been a strut in my step.

I was ushered up to the CEO's office to sit across a glass table from a kind-
faced, older gentleman named David. As he regaled me with his delight over
acquiring my business, I peeked at the office's many photos of David with
politicians—presidents, senators, and congressmen, all men, all Republicans—
and the many stuffed elephants tucked alongside the frames, presumably gifts
from those important men for various favors and donations. This was long
before the political vitriol of the current day, and while I know and love many
open-hearted conservatives, I had made my career squarely on the other side
of the aisle.

I was not represented on David's shelves.

No matter, I thought.

My pantyhose and I pressed on.

David talked about some "slight changes" to my firm's approach
and some "strategic redirection" of our founding principles. He glossed over
the values that underpinned every piece of what my company did in his haste
to get to the bottom line: he thought we'd achieved success through some sort
of voodoo magic.

It was the usual mild misogyny and slight condescension, unintentional
and benevolent—nothing I hadn't experienced a million times already from
other kind-faced, older sorts. By this point in my career, I'd gotten good
at smiling through it.

But I was not represented in David's words.

No matter, I thought.

My pantyhose and I pressed on.

He spoke of how my small business would be brought into the fold
of his much larger company, about how we would naturally need to make certain changes aligned with his view of the work and of the world, and the steps

---

1 *fapitzed*, adj., Yiddish: looking one's best; fancy; dressed to kill; or (in my nana's case)
presentable enough to be introduced to a nice Jewish doctor.

and the timeline required for me to undo precisely what made the company unique—what made it special—before I would be quietly excused out the side door, and my people, my clients, my processes would become wholly his.

I was not represented in David's plans.

No matter, I thought.

My pantyhose and I again pressed on.

I was supposed to want this—the path that was less scary, more traditional, with real money guaranteed. But something just didn't feel right.

At long last, the conversation turned to dollars. David took a folded piece of paper out of a portfolio and, as if we were in an old-school movie, slid it across the glass table. "I'm very excited to take your little company to the place of its fullest potential," he said.

I looked down at the piece of paper and, through the crystal-clear table, caught sight of my legs suffocating in their pantyhose prison. Then it dawned on me exactly what felt wrong: I'd made a special trip to the store to buy pantyhose for the occasion of selling my soul to its very first suitor.

I didn't even want a suitor, yet I'd put on a new pair of pantyhose for him nevertheless.

It would all be so simple, though. All I needed to do was unfold that piece of paper, read a number, and surf the waves of five years' struggle all the way to the bank. All I needed to do was sign on the bottom line.

But I was still looking at the pantyhose.

So I looked up and said, "Thank you for your interest, but I think I'll be the one to take my company to the place of its fullest potential."

I didn't sign on the bottom line. I never even unfolded that piece of paper.

No matter, I thought.

Instead, my pantyhose and I walked out the door.

Be Limitless

Walking out of that fancy downtown office in my fancy pantyhose—but without that fancy folded piece of paper—was when I decided to start dreaming bigger. Before I'd walked in the door, I had an idea of what my future could be: get acquired, make a little money, fade into the sunset. But sitting in that office, I realized I had built a company based on my own very specific definition of success. And this sale, no matter how lucrative it might be, was going to fly in the face of everything I held dear.

David wanted to prioritize the maximization of profit; I had started my firm to maximize personal flexibility and impact in the world. As I describe in my previous book, *Limitless: How to Ignore Everybody, Carve Your Own Path, and Live Your Best Life*, any leader, manager, or entrepreneur must think about these three factors—profits, flexibility, and impact—and make decisions based on one or (at most) two of those factors. It is impossible to start or run a business based on all three. But if you stick with your two main priorities, the third will eventually follow.

Sitting in that swanky office, I realized this same disconnect over values was the reason I'd left the big marquee firm where I'd started my career. It may not have felt this way to everyone, but the underlying message I got from my managers was: *Profits first. Client impact second. And what even is personal flexibility?*

This message didn't comport with who I am. I was not in *consonance*, so I quit that firm and started my own. And that firm of mine grew to a size that meant David wanted it. But he didn't understand that what made our firm different—putting our employees and our clients in front of our profits—was what made us wildly profitable. Being in consonance allowed me to be fully and unapologetically me.

Consonance is the central idea of *Limitless*. Perhaps you have read it, but it bears a brief revisit here because finding your Wonderhell rests upon an essential goal—being intertwined with who you are at your core and what you hold most dear.

So, here's the skinny.

We all have a similar goal: We want success to feel meaningful. We want our work to matter. But it doesn't, and we feel stuck, no matter how hard we hustle and grind toward success or how much we achieve it. That's because the problem isn't how we achieve success; it's how we define it.

Each one of us, at some point in our lives, was given a scorecard—a checklist, if you will—that defined success. You might have gotten yours from a teacher, a parent, a coach, a friend, a boss, a personal hero, or even an internet celebrity—or maybe you don't even remember how you got it. But it has been tucked in your back pocket for as long as you can recall, demanding that you fill in all the right checkboxes of generally accepted, externally defined success. You fill and fill and fill, but you still end up feeling empty.

Here's why: You can't be insatiably hungry for, deeply inspired by, or happily fulfilled by someone else's goals. For your working life to *feel* right for you, it has to actually *be* right for you. And that scorecard? It has nothing to do with you.

Instead, what if you pursued consonance—that sensation of alignment and flow that comes when *what* you do matches *who* you are? Consonance is made up of four elements:

> *Calling* is a gravitational pull toward a goal larger than yourself—a business you want to build, a leader who inspires you, a societal ill you wish to remedy, a cause you desire to serve.

> *Connection* gives you sightlines into how your everyday work serves that calling by solving the problem at hand, growing the bottom line, or reaching that goal.

> *Contribution* is an understanding of how this job, this brand, this paycheck contributes to the community to which you want to belong, the person you want to be, or the lifestyle you'd like to live.

> *Control* reflects how you influence your connection to that calling, in order to have agency in your work (that is,

in the assignment of projects, deadlines, colleagues, and clients), offer input toward shared goals, and contribute to your career trajectory and earnings.

Everyone, at every age and every stage, wants and needs these four elements—calling, connection, contribution, and control—in different amounts. Your definition of *consonance* will be different from mine.[2] Plus, how you experience consonance today will be different from your experience ten years ago and ten years from now.

But once you begin working toward the wonderful goal that is so meaningful to you, you'll find it's the one to trigger that hell because, this time, you actually care. Finding Wonderhell means finding that meaningful goal, and this requires doing some things differently.

First, you'll want to ignore everyone else's definitions of success and create your own. And second, you'll want to start dreaming in elephants.

Dream in Elephants

Did you know that it takes two years to gestate an elephant, but only nine weeks to birth a litter of puppies?

So, a dog could bear litter after litter after litter of puppies, but the elephant? Yep, still pregnant. Some things are just so big, it takes more effort and resourcefulness to conceive them. And while you might be fond of playing among scores of cute little puppies—hello, bucket list!—if you're trying to do something big, something ground-shaking, something worthy of your potential, bringing a few poodle-sized ideas into the world might not be enough. You're going to want to dream in elephants.

David Usher is no stranger to dreaming in elephants. Lead singer of Moist—one of the most successful bands ever to come out of Canada—and now a pioneer in the educational artificial intelligence (AI) space, David has always imagined a world that others couldn't yet see, whether it was cre-

---

2 If you need help finding your own definition of consonance, go to LimitlessAssessment.
com and take our twenty-minute, deep-dive assessment.

ating melody and lyrics out of whole cloth or conceiving technology that has not yet been built. He's also had to contend with no one understanding what he's saying.

"When I describe to people what we're going to build—say, an AI rendering of Albert Einstein holding an interactive discussion on the theory of relativity with schoolchildren—they all nod and smile at me," David explains. Later, he would hear about what happened after he left the meeting room. "They all looked at each other strangely and asked, 'What the fuck was he even talking about?'"

Perhaps that scenario of feigned understanding seems familiar to you. Perhaps you are managing a team, pushing them to achieve what they never could imagine for themselves. Perhaps you are pushing yourself, not 100 percent certain that what's on the other side even really exists. You are living through a chaotic, creative, ambitious moment, trying to dream things that are bigger than anyone else can yet envision.

No one is naturally comfortable in this scenario. As David points out, everyone and everything (even you) will try to beat your idea into submission, to make it more comfortable, until it becomes a boring, normal-size thing that we've all seen before.

"We get beaten down by the realities of technology and life and money, and all these things we need to make stuff happen," he says. "But you want your dream to be big enough that even after all this beating down, it still has value to you in its conclusion."

Unfortunately, though, this is where most people off-ramp. After experiencing frustration or a dead end, they drop out of the process and never achieve their most creative work. And that's what separates what David calls, in his book *Let the Elephants Run*, the "one-time creative" from the "lifetime creative": the willingness to get comfortable being uncomfortable, just as David has done in his own journey from musician to technology mastermind. Those who can revisit Wonderhell again and again know that in the difficulty, in the struggle, in the failure—in the willingness to dream big—we become our best, most creative selves.

When people can't internalize your vision, it feels like failure. But this type of failure is how you know you're experimenting with new capabilities, pushing past boundaries, and taking enough chances. If you aren't failing at least a little, are you even really trying?

So, accept that failure will happen sometimes. Don't let it signal doom. The road hasn't dead-ended; your story is not done. It has just started getting interesting.

Opportunity opens its doors only for those bold enough to walk through them—for those who give themselves permission to be ambitious.

Permission to Be Ambitious

Sallie Krawcheck decided to dream bigger after an aha moment one morning while putting on her makeup. She looked into the mirror—one eye shut, mouth ajar, mascara wand in hand—and thought, *The retirement savings crisis is actually a women's crisis.*

Compared with men, Sallie reasoned, working women in this country earn less, are expected to take more unpaid family leave, end up carrying more debt, and are not encouraged as strongly to invest. Yet she knew that women live six to eight years longer than men do, requiring a longer retirement horizon—and that 80 percent of women die single. The gender pay gap is an issue, and a big one, but by Sallie's estimation, this is compounded by the *faux-empowerment* way we talk to women about money.

Most media messages targeting women are either fearmongering (*Money is hard!*) or patronizing (*Maybe if you could just resist that crème brûlée latte or skip the avocado toast!*). Cue *Sex and the City*'s Carrie Bradshaw buying too many shoes and not being able to afford her apartment. *Oops!* Male-facing media messages, on the other hand, encourage every last Mr. Big to buy the T-bone steak and the fancy car. When money lessons for men are all about power, strength, and independence, perhaps it's no coincidence that 99 percent of investment dollars are managed by companies owned by men.

Sallie wasn't just some random person musing about the economic status of women all around the planet, but a bona fide financial whiz. Back in high school, when all she was thinking about was her cute jock boyfriend, a guidance counselor pulled her aside and pointed to her SAT scores and IQ test results. "You can write your own ticket," the counselor advised. "Do you want to be hanging on the smile of a football player, or do you want to see what you can do?"

Suddenly, Sallie had permission to be ambitious. She rode that ambition like a rocket ship, from a research analyst role at Sanford C. Bernstein & Co., where she pushed to take the company out of lucrative but conflict-rich deals and landed herself on the cover of *Forbes* as "the last honest analyst" in the process, to leadership at Citigroup, where she was recruited as chief financial officer and later head of the Smith Barney unit. "I went from managing two hundred eighty-six people on a Wednesday," Sallie recalls, "to forty thousand people on a Thursday."

On the home front, Sallie was also managing two children, two stepchildren, two cats, and a husband, and could easily put herself in the shoes of her female investors who worried about short-term risk, long-term gain, and how each decision would play out in their own portfolio. Her calculated, judicious, measured way of thinking didn't jibe with the fast and loose ways that Wall Street tends to play. And when she stood her ground on issues that mattered to her, Sallie was fired—twice, in fact, and both times in stories on the front page of the *Wall Street Journal*.[3]

But on that fateful morning, while applying mascara and thinking about the retirement savings crisis, her next thought was: *What if someone built an investment business by women, for women?*

The person capable of building and running such a business, Sallie figured, would need a deep financial background, like that of a research analyst. She would have to be contrarian, capable of looking at things differently. She would need to be able to assemble and manage a top-notch tech team, and be credible and connected enough to raise a lot of money from venture

---

3 David Enrich, "Krawcheck Is Leaving CitiGroup: Wealth-Unit Chief Exits Amid Tension With CEO Pandit," *Wall Street Journal*, September 23, 2008; Dan Fitzpatrick and Robin Sidel, "BofA Shakes Up Senior Ranks," *Wall Street Journal*, September 7, 2011.

capital firms that don't typically fund women in fintech. And she would probably have to be someone who had experienced—and endured—public failure.

"What person has a chance in hell of doing that?" she asked herself.

And she heard herself answer back, "You."

Everything Sallie had done up until that point was proof that she could play bigger, with her own brand of success. And in 2014, she founded Ellevest—an investment platform by women, for women. As of 2021, under Sallie's leadership, Ellevest was managing more than $1.5 billion.

Sometimes that all-important aha moment comes in the back of a rickety band van. Sometimes it comes across a fancy conference table. And sometimes it comes when you're putting on mascara. Regardless of when lightning strikes, give yourself permission to dream bigger and bolder. Bat those lashes, baby! Embrace this new you.

ARE YOU READY FOR THIS RIDE?

You were quite content with your past triumphs and accomplishments until you stepped into the Imaginarium and saw it: the *you* that you want to be, the life that you want to live, the potential that you want to fulfill. Now you can't unsee it. So, what are you going to do with the burden of your potential—this ambition, this Wonderhell?

I say, get all up in its business and have a ball!

That life you want is right there on the other side of your decision, waiting for you to believe it can be yours. All you have to do is let yourself play bigger in the Imaginarium. Accept the challenge of living up to the new you. Rather than apologizing for what you want, live fully into this new opportunity. Grab hold of past failures that will instruct future growth. Trade fear and regret for something new: adventure.

As you begin to reflect on your newfound potential, struggling under the weight of its burden, consider the following questions:

- What is your definition of success, and what goals within that definition compel you?
- When have you felt the heart-fluttering excitement and flow of doing what you love?
- What whispered goals do you have, even if you aren't sure they are possible or don't feel brave enough to speak them aloud?

Making Your Own Luck

★

Come sit at the Fortune Teller's table . . . she's been waiting for you! Peer into the crystal ball as she conjures forth magical secrets and reveals your destiny. What, you thought some people were just born blessed? With the help of this clever clairvoyant, you'll realize how to make your own luck, hone your intuition, and manifest everything you've ever wanted.

Building a House, Building a Home

Cara Brookins expected that the muscle-bound man she married would protect her. What she didn't expect was that his severe paranoid schizophrenia would lead to years of abuse, fear, and stalking.

Cara struggled every day just to survive, employing a series of baby steps that would keep her and her children safe. They pushed dressers in front of their doors at night. They kept their heads down and avoided eye contact. They stopped relaxing, laughing, communicating.

"One morning, I was driving the kids to school—being one of those real overachiever moms, warming my two-year-old's blueberry Pop-Tart with the car's heating vent—and I saw my kids in the rearview mirror," she recalls. "I saw their slumped shoulders, their haunted eyes, and their small, small futures. I decided right then and there that we had spent too much time edging down the path toward mere survival. We were done with all these failed little baby steps."

Cara had to make a radical move, one that would change her family's entire trajectory. She and her children needed to find a safe place—a new, inexpensive home to live in. And she had just the "big, crazy idea" to do it: they would build their own house. But they wouldn't just build it the way a normal family would, by hiring an architect, a contractor, a plumber, an electrician. No, they were going to build their future with their own bare hands.

When the idea first popped into Cara's head, she jumped on it. This project was so big, so crazy that Cara hoped it might solve an even more essential problem. "It was the first spark of something bigger," she says. "We were going to do something that would forever change the way we saw ourselves and what we were capable of."

Cara was a mother of four working full time, writing computer code for eight hours a day. The only thing she had ever built before was a bookcase. "I figured this would be the same, like a slightly larger IKEA project," she laughs.[1] "But seriously, we knew it would be more difficult than a normal family project. But we weren't a normal family. We had been through hell."

As they started to build, the family discovered what it was like to put in twenty-hour days of hard physical labor, but they also discovered something else: "the first hint that we could take physical action," as Cara explains, "to literally build ourselves a better life."

Each morning, Cara and her children—ages seventeen, fifteen, eleven, and yes, two!—would go to the construction site where they had dumped fifteen hundred concrete blocks, a mountain of two-by-fours and pipes, and piles of nails, along with their entire life savings and a looming foreclosure deadline on a small bank loan. They were armed with plastic bags around their tennis shoes, pails and shovels, a handful of hobby-level tools, and the knowledge that they had Googled and YouTubed the night before.

---

1 Before you get too excited, it turns out that IKEA doesn't sell 3,500-square-foot houses with five bedrooms, three bathrooms, a floor-to-ceiling library, a three-car garage, and a two-story treehouse.

It seems they weren't alone: "How to run a gas line without blowing yourself up" has about 42.7 million queries.

Cara and her children woke up every single day faced with uncertainty, doubt, and fear. But each day they made a little progress, pouring concrete, laying the foundation, framing walls, and building even more bookcases. Each day they saw possibility grow before their eyes. Each day they, too, grew. They began to communicate with each other again, to laugh, and to dream.

"My kids and I came out the other side of trauma thinking the most important thing we needed was this place to live," Cara says now. "But the story, our story—it was never about a house. It was this process of building a house together that taught us how our determined family can turn trauma into power and fear into courage, as proof that we can all build ourselves a life without limits."

Cara and her children didn't just build a house; they built a home. And they did it by using their own muscles and making their own luck.

Let's Get Lucky

We all know people who appear to magically, easily, always get what they want. And we also know people who just seem cursed—opportunities never seem to break their way, and things just don't work out for them. Some people are just lucky, and others are unlucky, and there's not much we can do to build the life we want. Right?

Well, not exactly.

Good fortune isn't just determined by fate. Some people do things that put them in a position to create what we call "good luck," while others do the opposite and create what we call "bad luck." And onboarding certain mindsets, outlooks, energies, and traits can help you build good luck into your life.

The four factors that make someone lucky, according to Dr. Richard Wiseman in his 2003 book, *The Luck Factor*, are:

- creating and noticing chance opportunities,
- listening to intuition,

- having positive expectations, and
- adopting a resilient attitude that turns bad outcomes into good outcomes.

So, it doesn't matter whether you've been "unlucky" in the past, or whether you attribute past success to nothing more than a random stroke of luck. You can create your own luck starting today, just like Cara did, to match your newfound potential.

Michelle Poler did exactly this when she created the 100 Days Without Fear project, challenging herself to do something every single day that scared her. She jumped out of an airplane. She started a dance party in Times Square. She did stand-up comedy. She quit her job. But how did she go from being afraid of everything to tackling some of the biggest fears that we all share? She made herself lucky.

First, she created and noticed opportunities for chance encounters by forcing herself to act like an extrovert. (Fellow raging introverts, I see you twitching, and I'm twitching, too. Stick with me for a minute.) According to Dr. Wiseman, extroverts are "luckier" than introverts because they put themselves out into the world. They try on a new persona for size and refuse to think of themselves as impostors. They smile more, strike up conversations with strangers, notice fresh possibilities, and work to keep their networks warm. This puts them top-of-mind and tip-of-tongue when opportunities arise. It puts them directly in the deal flow.

Second, Michelle listened to her intuition—all of her intuition. In the past, she only heard her neuroses and anxieties listing all the things that could go wrong. But then she decided to embark on this endeavor of choosing to believe—yes, you can!—that things would work out. Michelle made a list of everything that scared her and stopped asking, *What's the* worst *that can happen?* Instead, she asked, *What's the* best *that can happen?* By shifting her focus, she was able to hear the rest of her intuition, which sensed promise and hope in each frightening opportunity.

Third, she expected positive outcomes and taught herself how to *feel* lucky. Michelle cultivated a state of optimism and openness to new people, new ideas, new experiences. Expecting good fortune fattens the pipeline of potential inputs, which leads to additional possibilities—for instance, by increasing your chances of running into someone who holds opportunity in their hands. And having positive expectations leads to self-fulfilling prophecies, such as Michelle's meteoric rise in the media and as a motivational speaker, and her best-selling book *Hello, Fears*, which details all one hundred days and what she learned in the process.

Fourth, Michelle developed resilience by changing her mindset about failure, choosing to see it as a learning opportunity on the path to something bigger and better. She learned how to deny that her previous fate of embarrassment and fear was the inevitable future. Setting the expectation of being lucky turned bad luck into good fortune by simply transforming her view of the failure from a dead end into part of the process.

Being extroverted, open-minded, optimistic, and resilient won't really make you any luckier. These traits just prepare you to take advantage of the opportunities and lessons that come your way. Grit and resilience come when you laugh in the face of failure, knowing the lessons learned will help you reach a happy result eventually. Striving to exist in this state of mind—along with continued, concerted effort—is what brings you success, even though to the outside world it looks a whole lot like luck.

But even if being extroverted, open-minded, optimistic, or resilient is not native to your personality—as it wasn't to Michelle at the start of her 100 Days Without Fear—you can adopt these character traits as a situational "luck tourist." That's what I do.

Smile at people. Make eye contact. Practice positive affirmations. Start conversations. Focus on the lessons learned. Say yes whenever you can. Reconnect with your network. Choose a placebo talisman. And most important, expect that good things will happen, because they will.

Your inner voice says so.

Your Inner Voice Has Seen Some Shit

You know that voice that whispers, sometimes from out of the blue, *That guy's a creep*, or *This is the right business to start*, or *That candidate is the ideal one to hire*? That's your intuitive voice, and you probably trusted it to help you climb to the pinnacle of your most recent success. Now, as you face your next challenge, you should trust it again—even if you can't always hear it clearly.

Just as you can make yourself luckier by acting as a lucky person acts, you can improve your intuition by listening to it more closely. Because with all you've been through up to this point, your inner voice has seen some shit. You just need to get better at hearing it, and that means blocking out the other voices in the chorus that constantly assault your ears.

Other people's views, accounts, and predictions often serve up an easy platter of ready-made opinions before we manage to form a perspective ourselves. Uncertainty, indecision, anxiety, neuroses, and the all-pervading impostor syndrome fuel our desire to opinion-shop, trying on one soothsayer's notion after another until we find one that fits. Except that's a cop-out.

Why crowbar your discombobulation of unformed feelings into someone else's neatly packaged, prefabricated opinion? Instead, spend some time in the discomfort of the unknown, chewing things over with your own teeth while asking your inner psychic that tough question: *How do I really, truly feel?*

Divining the answer requires that you ignore the naysayers crowding out your intuition—echoes of all the people who claim that they know better than you. Those voices make you question your instincts. But your instincts got you to where you are today, didn't they?

Not only that—those instincts were perfected over millions of years of evolution! Don't believe me? Look in the mirror. Your gene pool survived this long, and it's not just because your ancestors outran the mastodon. It's because their inner voice told them the mastodon was already thundering their way.

Make a list of what your intuition has told you over the years whenever there was a big decision to make: the doubts you had about someone, the risk you chose to take, the route that just looked wrong, the dream you refused to let die.

Next, recall the stressful upheaval leading up to that big decision—and the wash of relief you felt the minute you chose a path forward, no matter how scary that path might have been. That's your intuition sighing a giant *phew!* That's how you really, truly feel. And if that relief never comes? Well, then you know you've made the wrong choice.

Now ask yourself: *Am I better or worse for having listened to my inner psychic?* My bet is that even if things didn't work out as you expected, the lessons you learned have informed and equipped you for the next thing, and the thing after that, and the thing after that.

We hear all the time from successful people who've listened to the voice of intuition. "Trust your instincts," the inimitable Oprah Winfrey once wrote in her eponymous magazine. "Intuition doesn't lie." Usually, that voice comes in the form of a question, such as:

Are you sure you should be dating her?

Don't you think you could do your boss's job better than he does?

Does this risk really feel right to you?

What if now is the time to buy?

In exploring questions that arise from deep within, you will uncover the data and knowledge that will lead you to make better decisions—in effect, to foretell your own fortune and manifest your own destiny.

Sort of.

Demystifying Manifestation

I've got good news and bad news about manifestation, that mythical belief that we can dream something into existence if we just think about it hard enough. I don't want to disappoint you, but here's the bad news: You're not going to conjure up the partner of your dreams simply by hoping they'll show up. You won't land the job of a lifetime just by expecting it. That sweet, cherry-red Maserati is not going to appear in your driveway simply because you've cut out a photo and attached it with glitter tape to your bedroom mirror—at least, not in the way you expect.

Don't fret! Here's the good news: the very act of thinking about what you want brings your desires within reach. Paying attention to your inner voice—and having an active dialogue with it—is how manifestation works. It's why vision boards work. It's why the law of attraction works. In other words, it's the secret behind *The Secret*.[2]

Think about any time you've ever hummed a song only to hear it on the radio soon thereafter. Or all those times you've thought about ordering Korean food for dinner only to start noticing social media posts about kimchi. You're not bending the universe, manifesting these things like a newly minted graduate of Hogwarts. Nor are you an undiscovered oracle, envisioning trivial moments in the future. You simply have told your conscious mind—which can process only fifty bits of information per second—to actively seek out this one additional bit of the eleven million bits hurled at it with each tick of the clock.[3]

Telling yourself you want something doesn't mean you'll just get it, but you'll get something else instead. Suddenly you'll see doors opened, invitations given, and offers extended that make the object of your desire all the more possible. Were these doors opened, invitations given, offers extended before? Possibly yes. But did you see them? Probably no. You simply weren't attuned to them. Maybe you weren't ready. Maybe you weren't interested. Or maybe you told yourself—in the full-throated, unambiguous terms that doubt always manages to speak so confidently—you didn't deserve them.

But here's the even better news about manifestation: The very process of engaging in this intentional practice actually makes you better at the thing that scares you. The more you observe and absorb information about a potential change, the more you begin to understand how to make that change happen. In this way, your awareness of the potential change makes the actual change come about more quickly, more naturally, and more successfully than it otherwise would.

---

2 This influential 2006 film and self-help book by Rhonda Byrne introduced the "law of attraction" concept to the modern world.
3 Encyclopedia Britannica Online, "Applications of Information Theory: Physiology," accessed August 24, 2022, https://www.britannica.com/science/information-theory/Physiology.

So how do you notice the doors, invitations, and offers that were there all along?

Indulge me for a moment while I get a little woo-woo on you, and let's talk about the difference between intuition and psychic powers. While the terms are often bandied about interchangeably, *intuition* is the unconscious processing of primary sensory information, while *psychic ability* is the processing of extrasensory perception of inputs that aren't so obvious.[4] Each is employed in the service of decision-making, but with intuition, you can point to a fact pattern that validates the feelings that support your decision. With psychic ability, it's not so clear. And this is where we move beyond what we learned in high school biology.

Humans are trained to attend to the five senses—taste, smell, sight, touch, and hearing—and have ignored what some argue might be many, many more. Have you ever sensed temperature? That's thermoception. What about pain? That's nociception. What about balance? That's equilibrioception. What about awareness of your body? That's proprioception.

I could go on and on; some studies point to as many as fifty-three senses.[5] But the point is this: Some of the sensory information our bodies receive every single second can be attributed to more than just a few senses. And awakening ourselves to more inputs—opening up our psychic ability to receive and interpret the intangible bits of information by instructing certain bits of data to bubble up to the surface—makes our intuition that much stronger. Training ourselves in this way would allow us to notice when what we want is actually right there in front of us.

But if manifestation isn't working for you, just turn out your inner drag queen.

---

4 Definitions from *Psychic Witch: A Metaphysical Guide to Meditation, Magick, and Manifestation* by Mat Auryn.
5 The Sensory Trust, a nonprofit authority on sensory design, references several such studies.

We're All Born Naked, and the Rest Is Drag

Jackie Huba was as surprised as anyone to meet Lady Trinity, which is saying something since Lady Trinity had lived inside of her forever.

Jackie was working in marketing, enjoying an upwardly mobile career first at IBM and then at boutique marketing firms, where she helped brands turn fans into fanatics. She had authored four books and toured the world as a professional speaker. She was good at this work, but she'd done it for many years, and it no longer felt groundbreaking or fresh. She was playing small, just letting life happen to her. Then one evening, she turned on the television to find the popular show *RuPaul's Drag Race*, and she couldn't tear her eyes away.

The drag queens she saw on the show were larger-than-life figures, unabashed and unafraid, creating their own destiny. They radiated a sense of self that was the opposite of how Jackie felt. At forty-seven years old, Jackie had achieved great things, but she still lacked the bold confidence she had expected to earn by that point.

As RuPaul often says, "We're all born naked, and the rest is drag." Jackie couldn't help but wonder if she, too, was just in a different form of drag: wearing a certain suit, expressing a certain personality, fitting herself into a certain box for the approval of friends, family, coworkers, and clients. But the drag queens on television? They didn't worry about being impostors. They didn't try to fit in. They stood out!

Jackie began to study drag queens and how they discovered and fully embodied these giant personalities. Most important, she explored whether the rest of us could do it too. She captured what she learned in her book *Fiercely You: Be Fabulous and Confident by Thinking Like a Drag Queen*—but first, she had to become a drag queen herself.

Jackie jumped directly into the sequined bodysuit, the giant wig, the fabulous makeup, and the theatrics. She even got herself some backup dancers. (Pro tip: Always, always, always have backup dancers.) This isn't your usual hustleporn, fake-it-'til-you-make-it nonsense. Jackie wasn't planning to use Lady Trinity to *fake* who she wanted to be. She wanted to *find* who she had been all along.

You've heard of music therapy and art therapy? Jackie went to drag therapy. Being Lady Trinity allowed Jackie to access that person she already was—that fabulous Jackie she had never allowed to surface. Once outed, however, Lady Trinity told Jackie that she had even bigger plans.

Lady Trinity was going to help Jackie make her own luck.

It just so happened that Lady Trinity was born at about the same time Jackie became righteously indignant about the state of United States politics. After a lifetime of political involvement that only included voting once every four years, she looked around for something she could do to make a difference. Then she learned that during the 2016 presidential election, one in five LGBTQ+ people was registered to vote—and more than one hundred million people did not vote at all.

Jackie knew marketing. She knew community activation. And she realized that she was the one to get this voting bloc to the polls.

When Jackie started Drag Out The Vote—a nonpartisan nonprofit that would register voters right at drag shows—her plan was to start small, raise a little bit of money, register a few voters. But after she shared her relatively humble goals, Lady Trinity yelled, "You need to go bigger! This can be huge!"

That's when Jackie's wonder ran smack into her hell.

She was terrified. She'd never done anything like this before. Jackie had never worked in either politics or the nonprofit world. But Lady Trinity was using her makeup palette to paint an unignorable picture in Jackie's mind. And in that moment, Jackie knew she would never again be satisfied sitting back and waiting for great things to just happen.

Since founding Drag Out The Vote in 2019, Jackie's team has raised $175,000, recruited 303 drag ambassadors in forty-four states, and contacted nearly half a million voters via text—and even more through the organization's 1.2 billion media impressions in 113 markets and 7.8 million social media hits.

And Jackie's day job? Because of her connections with Drag Out The Vote, she now brings real passion to work every day with a talent management firm she founded, Fiercely You Entertainment, representing some of the biggest drag artists in the business.

Jackie made her own luck by allowing herself to dream bigger, believing the fantasy even before she made it a reality. And she brought this dream to life with the unapologetic power and support of Lady Trinity.

And her backup dancers, of course.

ARE YOU READY
FOR THIS RIDE?

To get what you want from your next Wonderhell, you'll need to work really hard and get really lucky—and you'll find that getting extra lucky happens naturally when you're working extra hard. With the Fortune Teller on your side, it's possible not only to envision your best future but to engineer your fate.

No one is born lucky, but anyone can make their own luck. Be extroverted and optimistic whenever possible. Tune in to your intuition. Identify your goals, and keep an eye out for opportunities. Making your own luck is what got you to this current Wonderhell, even if you didn't realize it. What gets you to your next one will be no different because the only luck that exists is the luck you make yourself.

As you confront the reality of luck—looking for the promise of the future, but realizing that it's all up to you—consider the following questions:

- In what areas of your life could you act more extroverted, more open-minded, more optimistic, more resilient?
- What are your top goals for the next six, twelve, and eighteen months—and your big, hairy, audacious goals (BHAGs) for the next three to five years?
- How can you silence the voice of doubt and turn up the volume on your inner confidence?

THE HALL OF MIRRORS

Figuring Out Who You Are

★

Explore the Hall of Mirrors, that magic maze of truth and illusion, and see a whole new you! Search through the distorted reflections and competing realities for the real, transformed you—not the *you* from before, the one people said you were (or should be or must be), or even the *you* who got you here today, but the special you, the one who was made for more. Observe each disorienting looking glass, and come face-to-face with your true self—the person who will carry you to places beyond your wildest imagination. It's time to make friends with that new you.

Identity Is Not a Fixed Trait

Brandon Farbstein was born with metatropic dysplasia, an extremely rare form of dwarfism; there are fewer than a hundred known cases. Fully grown, at twenty-two years old, Brandon stands three foot nine inches.

"When I was four years old, I looked in the mirror and asked my mom why I didn't look like the kids around me. She told me that I had special bones and that they didn't grow in a way that other kids' bones do," he remembers. "That was the first time I had an image of myself as different."

And then the bullying began. Brandon would notice the way people reacted to him in public: the finger-pointing, the staring, the name-calling. By the time he was eleven, he had no sense of self—only an image created for him by others.

In 1902, the American sociologist Charles Horton Cooley coined the term "looking-glass self" to describe the tendency to base our sense of self on how we believe others perceive us. In other words, we aren't who we think we are, and we aren't who others think we are; we are who we *think* others think we are. As a result, our identity is shaped not individually but collectively. We imagine ourselves in this perceived but fixed looking-glass form rather than as malleable, ever evolving, and full of possibility. In the bargain, we give up the power to *choose* our identity, and therefore our future.

Brandon suffered keenly from this tendency. He felt alone, invisible, and unlovable, forever stuck in his looking-glass self—the way cruel strangers (and crueler classmates) saw him. Searching hard for self-acceptance, he found only self-loathing.

Then, at an airport one day when he was fifteen years old, everything changed.

"A woman came up to me and asked me about my Segway—it's part Transformer, part Lamborghini, and it works as my mobility device when I need to traverse long distances," he recalls. As they waited to board the same flight, she asked about his story. Then she shared hers: she was Hayley Foster, one of the original organizers of TEDx talks.

Brandon had spent the first decade and a half of his life hating that he was different from other people. But after talking to Hayley, he wanted to put himself out there, be transparent, and show people that everyone—regardless of who you are or how you are made—can feel alone, invisible, or unlovable, and that the best thing we can all do is have empathy for one another.

He soon signed on to do a TEDx talk. It was all of six minutes long, yet it changed the trajectory of his life. Suddenly he stopped asking, *Who am I? How should I act? What will other people think of me?*

After years of accepting the reflection of his identity from the wrong people, Brandon finally began to see himself for who he was and the value that he could bring to the world. Part of that value was serving as the driving force behind two new pieces of legislation signed into law in his home state, Virginia: one on bullying prevention and the other requiring all K–12 classrooms across the state to teach empathy and emotional intelligence.

Brandon learned that his identity isn't fixed by the gaze of others, but by what he sees for himself—his fuller, ever-evolving identity. With this brave new image reflecting back, he finally feels seen and loved for who he is.

But he still works every day on owning his identity.

"Working on seeing myself for who I truly am reaffirms to me that every part of me that is different and one-of-a-kind is special," Brandon says. "That's me, and I can either love that person fully and wholly and go forward as a beam of light—or step into that sense of self, and play small, and hide." Looking in the mirror now, he can see his own talents and gifts and offer some essential advice for the rest of us. "We need to unlock ourselves and recognize who we actually are and the potential that lies inside."

Borrow Confidence

Brandon found success when he stopped letting others assign his identity and figured it out on his own. This gave him the confidence to evolve and change, to innovate and iterate, and to move forward as his true self. But how many of us are still attempting to be someone we're not, guided by the same terrible fake-it-'til-you-make-it advice? *I* sure was—especially in that Wonderhell moment of transitioning from an extensive career in recruiting into my current "bonus" career as an author and a speaker.

My story also involves a TEDx talk that I never expected (or wanted) to give. When I was first asked, in the fall of 2016, if I would be willing to speak my truth in front of 2,600 people, my initial response was "Hell, no! That's terrifying!" I'd never given a speech in public, and I wanted to keep it that way. But I was persuaded by my kids, who had withstood years of my motivational pep talks about doing the things that scared *them* most, to get up on that stage and do the thing that scared *me* most.

And get up on that stage I did—except I wasn't really me. Convinced it was best to hide my quirks and follow convention, I gave that first speech of my life as someone else: a robotic TED talker pretending to be someone I wasn't, reciting a script from memory and completely detached from the emotion it held. When I look back at that performance now, I cringe.

In April 2022, I was about to give another talk that terrified me, but this experience was entirely different. It would be my first live presentation after the worst of the COVID-19 pandemic had passed—my first time onstage, addressing thousands of real, live audience members after two years of talking into a camera from the comfort of my home, in the comfort of my pajamas. The audience was screaming and clapping, energized to finally be back at an in-person event. The DJ was thumping out beats. And the announcer started us off with one of those *Let's get ready to rummmmmmmble!* introductions.

Gulp.

A few weeks earlier, my friend Erin King, a successful author and speaker whom I admire, convinced me to ditch the script and speak from the heart about who I am, what I know, and how I came to know it. "Laura, you need to get up there and just *rant!*" she insisted, and she pointed out that I always post on social media about celebrities and luminaries standing proud and playing big while wearing their #limitlessyellow. "It's about time you did, too."

Double gulp.

It turns out that you can't play small in head-to-toe, bright Limitless Yellow. Yes, I strode out on the stage, channeling my best Amy Cuddy *power pose* and looking like a giant highlighter pen. And you know what? The crowd cheered wildly with love. That love gave me the courage to be bold. And my boldness was met with more love.

I let the clothes carry me forward, and holy cow! I preached potential, pride, and possibility for sixty straight minutes. I spoke with raw, reckless emotion, as if I didn't have a care in the world about what people thought of me. I told stories I'd never told before, with openness and honesty. And the audience was laughing, crying, and cheering all the way to the end, when the roar of five thousand screaming people on their feet blew my hair back—my first-ever standing ovation.

That's some outfit, right? From the outside, I'm sure I looked coura-geous and confident, strutting out to spread my message to the audience, undaunted, as if I knew what the hell I was doing. But like you, I was making it all up as I went along—and I still am. Every. Single. Big. Moment.

We often ascribe courage to people who look bold, who act bold, who dress bold. So, riddled with doubt and insecurity in front of this gigantic crowd, I tried on a new, bolder me. I borrowed confidence from my clothes, and then I borrowed confidence from the audience. And their energy gave me the cour-age to be even more confident. I channeled Todd Herman, author of *The Alter Ego Effect*, and the advice he uses with professional athletes, star perform-ers, and average joes—I thought about who I am when I'm at my very best. I thought about what part of me I needed to unleash so I could be that very best self on that stage. And then I let Laura take a seat and let loose my heroic alter-ego self: LGO.

And here's the thing I learned: I didn't have to be brave for the full sixty minutes. I just had to be brave for sixty seconds, letting them see and love the full me. That gave me the confidence to just be that true me going forward.

Kobe Bryant had Black Mamba.

Stefani Germanotta has Lady Gaga.

Jackie Huba has Lady Trinity.

And I have LGO.

Who do *you* catch sight of in the mirror—that most intoxicating, invigo-rating version of you?

When you reach for that brave vision, even just briefly, you can cross your own personal Rubicon and become unapologetically you.

Cross the Rubicon

While leading his soldiers across the Rubicon River to seize control of the Roman Republic in 49 BCE, Julius Caesar (legend has it) spoke the words *Alea iacta est*—Latin for "The die is cast." Anyone who has thrown craps in modern-day Vegas will recognize the truth in this metaphor. As soon as the dice have been thrown, even before they stop rolling, all bets are irrevocable. It's over. Your fate is sealed.

For Caesar and his men, crossing the Rubicon was the point of no return. The deed was done; there was no turning back. If they lost, they would be executed. But if they won—well, either way, nothing would ever be the same. There was the *them* before and the *them* after—forever changed.

Wonderhell is that Rubicon moment for you.

But Wonderhell is a sneaky bastard. You don't actually have to enter this new territory to be changed; you only have to glimpse it from the opposite side of the riverbank. The moment you catch sight of the other side and understand the larger battle is yours, if you want to fight—the moment you realize that your idea has legs, that it (and you) can be bigger—Wonderhell has got you. You've crossed your own Rubicon.

There is the *you* before and the *you* after—forever changed.

Sometimes this moment happens when you're sitting in the center seat on an airplane and a voice inside you suddenly insists you can do more. Sometimes it happens when someone slides a piece of paper toward you across a glass table. Regardless of *how* it goes down, the *what* is unmistakable: your side hustle wants to become your front-and-center obsession.

The die is cast.

This is decision time: Do you keep playing safe, nicking the edges, worrying about risk and how you might lose everything you've worked for until now? Or do you go all in and jump at the chance for breakthrough success? Do you choose the *you* that you've been or the *you* that you might become?

And once you choose to cross that river into what is possible, there is no going back. You can only go *through*. Each new Wonderhell becomes its own one-way journey.

So, how do you know if you've already crossed into Wonderhell?

Think about that bigger prize. Does your heart start to race? Do you daydream about the possibilities? Do you find your flow when you are working toward that larger idea? That's the wonder.

Has that idea gotten under your skin? Does it buzz like a fly in your ear? Does it pop up in all the strangest places and wave hello with that giant, shit-eating grin? Does it refuse to leave you in peace? That's the hell.

Sure, it scares you. But if your goals don't scare you at least a little bit, you've set the bar far, far too low.

You could run from this fear. You could hide from this future. You could lie to yourself about what you want. Many people do, swallowing that dream down into their belly, where it becomes a cancerous lament, festering away, disguised as malaise, dissatisfaction, or worse: prudence.

Let's just be careful, it warns.

Would you rather live with the fear of failure now or the despair of regret forever? Most people would tell you regret is indeed a cancer that infects every part of your life. And no one has ever lain on their deathbed thinking, *I wish I took fewer chances.*

One of the biggest regrets of those who are dying (according to Australian nurse and author Bronnie Ware, who spent years caring for patients in the final three months of life) is never crossing their personal Rubicon: "I wish I'd had the courage to live a life true to myself, not the life others expected of me."

Life is short. So, ask yourself, *What would I do if I dared to live a life true to me, true to all that I am capable of accomplishing?*

Are you going to apologize for who you really are, what you really love, and those big, hairy, audacious goals you really want to pursue? Or are you going to join Team No Regrets, hop into that boat, and cross the river into your next big thing?

And here's where Wonderhell sneaks up on you once again, because you already know what you want to do. Wonderhell only shows itself to the worthy—to those with the imagination to envision it there.

That's you. You're already here.

Impostor Syndrome: The Ultimate Gaslight

So, you've already started down that path to your next success by deciding to see yourself differently. But what if trying out your new identity makes you feel like an impostor?

Approximately 70 percent of us will experience impostor syndrome at some point in life.[1] Maybe, like me, you've feared that people will figure out you don't belong, you aren't worthy of the promotion, you aren't good enough to be in the room. And maybe, like me, you've cowered in the corner, afraid to take your shot, waiting for everyone else to wise up and call you a fraud.

Or maybe you took the opposite approach. You did your best to give off the impression that you belong, and unwittingly stirred up everyone else's insecurity: *You* act like you belong, and so *I* feel like more of an impostor. In response, *I* act like I belong even more, thereby making *you* feel even worse.

This phenomenon—where we push each other deeper into our respective impostor syndrome corners, never knowing what is really happening with the other person—is called *pluralistic ignorance*. It traps us in a perpetual, vicious, Academy Award–winning cycle of overcompensation, and it stinks. Rather than helping you get ahead, it's holding you back because it stops you from being you.

Impostor syndrome is gaslighting you.

I mean, just think about the gall of the terminology itself: The word *impostor* indicates *How dare you breach the walls of our safe space?* And *syndrome* implies *You must be ill—you should lie down!*

As the impostor, you have three options: You can hide who you are. You can change who you are. Or you can lose who you are. And each option just exacerbates that feeling of not belonging.

But perhaps the problem isn't with you at all. Perhaps being surrounded by manipulative mirrors is making you doubt your sense of reality, and the real problem is the world in which you are trying to operate.

The idea of impostor syndrome, as authors Ruchika Tulshyan and Jodi-Ann Burey explain, emerged in the 1970s, when leadership was far more

---

1 Jaruwan Sakulku and James Alexander, "The Impostor Phenomenon," *International Journal of Behavioral Science*, 2011.

homogeneous and the world was far less willing to acknowledge how people have to deal with racism, sexism, xenophobia, homophobia, and so forth. Yet the vestiges of victim shaming are rampant in the self-help mania that positions you, the so-called impostor, as the root cause. "Impostor syndrome puts the blame on individuals," Tulshyan and Burey write, "without accounting for the historical and cultural contexts that are foundational to how it manifests in both women of color and white women. Impostor syndrome directs our view toward fixing women at work instead of fixing the places where women work."[2]

In other words, when the very systems you operate in were built for people who don't look like you, act like you, think like you, pray like you, or love like you, it is impossible to cast off the feeling that you are an impostor. That doesn't make you inadequate. It makes the systems inadequate.

One particular quote bouncing around cyberspace (attributed falsely to Sigmund Freud, and probably spoken instead by an exasperated woman) perfectly sums up my advice to you: "Before you diagnose yourself with depression or low self-esteem, make sure that you are not, in fact, just surrounded by assholes."

You're not an impostor; you're an innovator. So, ignore those assholes, and pay attention to the voice that's been guiding you all along: your own.

Discovering the Power of Self-Talk

Dorie Clark hated childhood. She was lucky to come from a safe, loving home, but that didn't stop her from being angry. "I was angry that I wasn't allowed to vote, to have a job, to drive," she says now. "I just wanted to do all the things!"

One day, Dorie noticed a friend's mother reading a book by Tony Robbins. The mom couldn't wait to share his ideas, promising, "If you read this book at age thirteen, you're going to be unstoppable!" Dorie went home and dove right in.

2 Ruchika Tulshyan and Jodi-Ann Burey, "Stop Telling Women They Have Impostor Syndrome," *Harvard Business Review*, 2021.

What Tony Robbins did was translate Eastern concepts into Western terms, she points out now—not exactly a revelation for anyone who has studied Eastern philosophy. "But, hello! Being a thirteen-year-old in rural North Carolina, I had not, in fact, studied Eastern philosophy," Dorie says. It blew her mind to think that although you can't control many things that happen, you can control your *reaction* to those things.

"You can create your own way of interpreting the world that is more or less helpful to you," she recalls discovering. For a gay teenager with intellect and maturity well beyond her years, this was not just a revelation but a full-on *reveal* of who she could truly be.

With this mindset, Dorie left her rural hometown to attend college a year later, at age fourteen, and it served her well throughout her professional life as she reinvented herself over and over again. First she became a journalist, then a spokesperson for gubernatorial and presidential campaigns, followed by stints as a nonprofit executive director, a business school professor, an executive coach, a speaker, and the author of several best-selling books, including the aptly named *Reinventing You*. But Dorie's latest side hustle may be her most interesting reveal yet: learning to become a theater lyricist and Broadway investor. (Because that's an obvious career move, right?)

In this latest reinvention, Dorie had to summon up the courage to apply to one of the best musical theater writing programs in the country, the BMI Lehman Engel Musical Theatre Workshop. She was swiftly rejected. Dorie could have interpreted this as the finale, but instead she saw that it was just the intermission. (See what I did there?) She wasn't an impostor, unfit to be a student in the program. She was just not ready . . . yet.

So Dorie hired a coach, got down to work writing lyrics, and applied again—and this time she was accepted.

When she sat down on the first day, the student to her left had a master's degree in musical theater, and the student to her right had scored an entire show. Dorie had just three songs, but she refused to be intimidated. Inner confidence had become a lifelong habit, undergirding every reinvention and holding that negative self-talk at bay.

"For me, there was an early introduction to the fact that I had to be pretty solid with myself before I could telegraph any kind of self-confidence to other people," says Dorie. And she did exactly this when introducing herself at BMI that first day. Rather than thinking, *Oh shit, I'm in over my head*, before disappearing into her hoodie, she gave herself a familiar pep talk: *Okay, fortunately, you have really good self-esteem in other areas of your life*, she started out, *so you're not going to derive all your sense of worth from this unfamiliar experience.*

Maybe one day Dorie would become all that she dreamed of becoming, but in the moment, she recognized the hard truth: she wasn't very good. And that was okay. Dorie knew she wasn't very bad, either, and she was determined to try. Choosing to see that reflection of herself and her potential didn't make her an impostor. It just made her someone ready to live into this expanded vision of who she could be.

ARE YOU READY FOR THIS RIDE?

If standing on the edge of our incompetence makes us impostors, then I am an impostor. And so are you. Congratulations, and welcome!

Wandering through the Hall of Mirrors, you've glimpsed a new reality—a reflection of yourself and all that you can become. You are way outside of your comfort zone, a stranger on unfamiliar land, soaring past the voices that silence your potential. This is your new identity, provided you can shake off the old one that no longer fits.

Reimagine who you are! Take stock of your track record, and remind yourself that whatever practice got you here was good enough to open up this Wonderhell.

As you're coming to terms with the new you that has unexpectedly appeared, consider the following questions:

- What have you learned about yourself in the moments you felt like an impostor?
- In what ways is the voice inside your head holding you back, and how can you recalibrate so it cheers you forward instead?

- What have you done up until now that has set you up for what is to come?

Living into Your Truest Self

★

Right this way—the Tent of Oddities is next! Now you've seen the new you, but just how comfortable are you living fully into it? Are you ready to embrace the enigmatic you who's been hidden inside for eons? Enough with being scolded and molded! Here among the misfits, you'll learn what makes you different, what makes you special—and it's your turn to shine. When you accept and empower that bigger, better you, you can bring everything you *are* to everything you *do*.

Getting to Yes as You

Lydia Fenet was a college student when she picked up a copy of *Vanity Fair* magazine, read about an auction event celebrating Princess Diana, and fell madly in love.

The auction house: Christie's.

The auctioneer: proper, old, and English.

The guests: the best of New York society.

The black ties! The dresses! The glamour! Lydia could not get enough. *What even* is *Christie's?* she asked herself. *And how do I work there?*

With no clue about how hard it is to land a career-making internship in New York City, Lydia decided to simply call Christie's and ask about spending the summer working there. She reached the woman who ran the internship program and was immediately told that they had filled all thirty spots; there were no more openings. But Lydia didn't take no for an answer. She called back again and again, every single day, always getting the same answer to the same question. Eventually, she probed deeper, asking, "Why is the program capped at a specific number?"

"Interns go on field trips to museums all around New York City, and there is only so much space on these field trips," the woman replied.

So Lydia countered, "Well, what if I don't go on any of the field trips? Surely you need someone to stay back and answer the phones or make copies or do whatever interns do, right?"

Lydia spent that summer at Christie's. She didn't even miss a field trip, and she had the opportunity to shadow all the auctioneers to see how things were done. She watched them face thousands of people who were talking, drinking, and paying attention to anything but the auctioneers running the show, who were there to part them from their money. And she took careful notes on how those auctioneers—stiff, suited, and staid, right out of that *Vanity Fair* article—needed to command the room from the start.

Years later, when Lydia got her first auction assignment, she acted just like her role models. She wasn't old or English, but she sure could be proper. In she marched—stiff, suited, and staid like them. She was playing the role as it was modeled for her, fitting herself into the company's expectations, and it worked. Her auctions were successful, and she was instantly addicted to the thrill of the action. Still, she sensed that she was barely skimming the surface of what she could do.

Then one night, exhausted, exasperated, and super pregnant, Lydia cracked a self-deprecating joke onstage. The audience perked up, paid more attention, and most important, donated more money. Suddenly, Lydia's mind blew open with an idea: What if she acted less like a traditional auctioneer and more like her nontraditional self? Could she bring her charm, wit, and energy to make these events much more fun for the attendees—and much more lucrative for her nonprofit clients? Could she get auction-goers to bid, while starring in a brand-new role as herself?

Lydia dropped the prim and proper attitude and even developed her own "strike method"—marching up to the stage and banging her gavel three times on the podium—to command the room from the start.

Thwack! thwack! thwack!

"Good evening, ladies and gentlemen!" she announces. "My name is Lydia Fenet. Let's get down to business!"

By understanding who she truly is and embracing that whole self onstage, eccentricities and all, Lydia has raised over half a billion dollars for charitable causes at Christie's. And she did it not by being stiff, suited, or staid, but just by being herself.

The Meek Shall Inherit the Earth

Meek is not the first word anyone would use to describe me. And yet unlike Lydia, I identify as an introvert. Famous introvert Glennon Doyle once crawled inside of my brain and wrote: "I am a sensitive, introverted woman, which means that I love humanity but actual human beings are tricky for me. I love people but not in person. For example, I would die for you but not, like . . . meet you for coffee."

She is me.

What are we to do, then, when we figure out who we are, and that person isn't the type who likes to put themselves out there? What if playing bigger and making our own luck just isn't our natural state?

If you are an avowed introvert—or even if you're just feeling shy about putting yourself out there in some new way—you're not alone. One-half to two-thirds of us identify as introverts, according to Susan Cain, the author of *Quiet: The Power of Introverts in a World That Can't Stop Talking*. So look to your left, and then look to your right—at least one or two of those people is an introvert. (I know all you true introverts just read that sentence and laughed out loud, thinking, *There's no one next to me. I'm alone . . . duh!*) But when it comes to our professional lives, somehow we all get the message that we're supposed to be outgoing and uninhibited.

"Introverts are routinely passed over for leadership positions," Cain says in her TED talk, "even though introverts tend to be very careful, much less likely to take outsize risks—which is something we might all favor nowadays." Despite society's tendency to extol the virtues of extroversion, introverts, in fact, make better leaders.[1] Whereas extroverts more often put their own stamp on things, introverts can deliver superior outcomes because they are far more likely to give employees the freedom to run with fresh, diverse ideas.

I'm not here to harsh your buzz if you're an extrovert. I couldn't be happier for you (you socially well-adjusted weirdo!). Imagine the world without Leonardo da Vinci, Dr. Martin Luther King Jr., Margaret Thatcher, or Steve Jobs! We introverts thank you for your service (and also for how you "adopt" us, take us outside, and help us talk to real, live people). But while you might be the socially accepted norm, to some of us you're still incredibly foreign, just as we are to you.

Introverts and extroverts need each other. What's more, the world needs us both too. And we don't have to be just one or the other; being introspective or wary at times is just as natural as being a live wire. But if you're hesitant to step out of the shadows and show your truest self, remember that your inclination toward introversion often means you listen more and see more. You are probably more patient than other people. And you typically lead not out of ego, but out of the desire to build a better future.

Some of the most admired leaders throughout history—from Abraham Lincoln and Eleanor Roosevelt to Mahatma Gandhi and Rosa Parks— were introverts whose behavior did not conform to expectations. But being an introvert has a special power and worth of its own, Cain points out. "These leaders were at the helm not because they enjoyed directing others, and not out of the pleasure of being looked at," she continues. "They were there because they had no choice, because they were driven to do what they thought was right." This drive to do the right thing sometimes compels introverts to act like situational extroverts, playing the part of a showboat and reaping all the benefits that this outward-facing personality brings.

---

1 Adam Grant, Francesca Gino, and David A. Hoffman, "The Hidden Advantages of Quiet Bosses," *Harvard Business Review*, December 2010.

Regardless of how you identify, there is merit in each of these personas and everything in between. Just be true to yourself, whether you yearn for attention or stage left is your jam.

Maybe Stage Left Is Your Jam, Too

As someone who makes my living on the stage and in front of the camera, and who has learned to be unapologetic about who I am under that spotlight, I have a weird confession to make: I still hate center stage.

In fact, there is nowhere I'd rather be than stage left.

I spent the earliest part of my career working as a campaign staffer, helping get Bill Clinton elected president of the United States. I spent the next part of my career in the White House building AmeriCorps, which would enable more than a million young people to earn stipends for their college education while making their community a better place. Then I went into mission-driven executive search, where my job was to find incredible people and put them in positions where they could help make the world a better place.

Every one of those was a stage-left job—even the last one, where for fifteen years, I was the founder and CEO of a global executive search firm. Although I was often in the spotlight, it was my job to identify and amplify others, whether by recruiting incredible talent or as chief champion of my employees. Even in moments when I was forced to take center stage as CEO, I always redirected the spotlight to others, where it more aptly belonged.

I liked it there at stage left. It felt like home. Not only had I studied, recruited, stewarded, and coached leaders for the previous twenty years, but my first boss and mentor in the White House was Eli Segal, a man who never saw his name in the headlines, yet shaped history from the sidelines. Eli was a consummate stage-left leader—mild-mannered, not splashy—the sort who would be easy to underestimate. But he had a vision of the way the world should be, and he worked tirelessly behind the scenes to make it so. From a young idealist on Eugene McCarthy's failed 1968 bid for president to chief of staff on Bill Clinton's winning 1992 campaign, Eli was always making deals, connecting people, but never seeking the limelight.

After Eli's death, the *New York Times* dedicated a full page to his obituary. Memorials took place in Boston and Washington, DC. Senator Ted Kennedy gave the eulogy, saying, "There are over a thousand of you here today. Every one of you thinks that you were either Eli's best friend or Eli's very good friend . . . and every one of you is right." Eli wasn't the out-front leader, but people followed him everywhere.

Our conventional idea of leadership demands that the more we succeed, the more we get pushed to center stage—even if we don't like it there. We are thrust to the head of the table, when really the relationships and networking happen elsewhere. We are asked to speak more, so we end up listening less. This idealized, one-size-fits-all construct actually constructs worse leaders.

It is exhausting to be someone else. It's untenable. And it's never going to get you to the person you're meant to be.

Your leadership should look like you—a combination of your skills, interests, and energy, not to mention your quirks, moxie, and special brand of awkward. This might mean you occupy center stage sometimes, either literally or just metaphorically. But find a way to thrive there on your own terms, rejoicing in that moment as a lever to accomplish something even bigger. The spotlight may be on you, but the people you love, the causes you serve, and the businesses you build are the true stars of the show.

Be Unapologetic

My husband works with numbers. I work with words. But I also run a business, which means that every once in a while, I have to face a fear even more intense for me than public speaking: math.

It usually starts out with me banging my head against the desk over and over and over, trying to figure out something like a monthly average income, or a projected cash flow, or growth over time divided by the square root of the gravitational force of my will to live. An hour later, I finally give up and text him: HONEY, HOW DO I FIGURE OUT [insert highly complex, Einstein-level, *Beautiful Mind* math question here]?

And within four seconds and about ten keystrokes, he will reply with the answer, all bundled up in a Google-spreadsheet bow.

Ugh. I love him. I hate him.

To my husband, mathematical equations are as simple and ordinary as breathing. "It's just numbers," he says. "It's not that complicated." To me, though, it's basically magic. He might as well lift me out of my chair with a magic wand, twirl me around in the air, and return me to my seat, surrounded by doves flying out of top hats.

I am a writer. I write. To some, this might seem as magical as my husband's math skills seem to me. *Words are hard* and all that. But this is who I am; this is what I do. I'm not the best at it, but I'm somewhat better than average. I never thought much of my penchant for writing, other than the fact that it served me well in high school when I'd scribble off last-minute homework essays on the way to school in the morning. Still, some people look at me like I'm orchestrating a trick that has them levitating above *their* chair.

The world is a freak show, so why not celebrate our oddities? They make us who we are—and sometimes our idiosyncrasies are even instrumental in achieving our success. My husband is in the tent. I'm in the tent. And you, with your own talents and distinctions, are in here with us, too.

Everyone wants to be special, yet no one wants to be different. (Thanks for the life lesson, middle school!) But what if what makes us different is, in fact, what makes us special?

Think about your most recent success, or the last time someone complimented you or expressed admiration for something you did. Did you turn and say, "Oh, no, it's nothing! Anyone could do it"? Perhaps you did—it's a habit many people have. We are accustomed to deflecting and demurring, to reducing and revising, to belittling our talent because we don't want to seem arrogant. Even my husband, who got a perfect score on his math SAT a million billion years ago, dismisses his skill with a wave of his hand.

How would you behave if you were unapologetic about your talent?

There is a whole universe of space between *Oh, no, it's nothing!* and *I'm super awesome, the best ever to set foot on earth.* And finding that sweet spot—where you can admit to your talent and appreciate its value toward what you want to accomplish—is what will allow your impending future vision to flourish inside of you.

You can't push boldly into Wonderhell until you own your potential and your promise. There are things you have that others lack: your talents, your uniqueness, your magic. There are things you are willing to do that others are not: the work, the struggle, the discipline. Refusing to stifle these things is what separates people who reach for the expanded vision of their potential from those who never awaken to its gifts.

Yes, I get it. Sometimes it's uncomfortable to be unapologetic about your greatness, but remember: your greatness is not about you. Your greatness has a purpose—to solve problems for other people so they, in turn, can do more of what *they* do well.

Your greatness is that mirror that you hold up from your position at stage left.

Case in point: The only reason you are reading this book is that my husband's math wizardry regularly saves me from slow-impact, math-induced brain trauma, which frees up my time and my mental energy to work on writing. (*Thanks, hon.*) His gift became a gift to me, so I could bring my gift to you. And now you can bring your gift to the people in your life.

Living Out Loud

Anna Gomez had a secret. Although she worked as the chief financial officer with global advertising firm Leo Burnett, she had developed another career on the side. And that side career involved torrid love affairs and steamy sex.

Decades earlier, at age twenty-four, Anna had moved to Chicago from the Philippines with her husband, two small toddlers, and a handful of higher education degrees that did not impress hiring managers in the United States. She eventually found a job operating the copy machine at Leo Burnett and told herself that she would be satisfied just working her way up the ranks there. And she did, passing the CPA exam and earning her way into the top leadership.

Now she was successful, but unhappy living a life that didn't feel quite like her own. By day, Anna was helming the financial ship of one of the world's largest ad agencies, but by night, she was Christine Brae, romance novelist.

Christine Brae had published six novels, established a fan base, and built a dedicated following. Her books regularly stayed at the top of sales charts even months after their release. Her three most recent titles—*In This Life*, *Eight Goodbyes*, and *The Year I Left*—had won literary awards and were instant best sellers.

But she'd kept it all a secret.

"Nobody at Leo Burnett knew," Anna says. "I wasn't comfortable yet. I was building my career." She felt like there was something incompatible about being a CFO, upholding important corporate policies and procedures, while also being a romance writer. "I just couldn't reconcile the two," she explains. Plus, she kind of liked keeping things quiet.

Then one day Anna noticed how few women, especially women of color, were as high up in the financial industry as she was, and she realized that she had to get a little loud.

Anna began to speak out in a more public way. She started standing up—in meetings, in the media, on public stages—for different platforms, different beliefs, different identities. She became more vocal about issues affecting women in the workplace and the barriers they face when seeking to advance professionally. She spoke openly about the struggle of others just like her who were balancing work and family obligations, and who felt they had to leave part of themselves at the door every day. As she called attention to how those women could be happier as their fullest selves, she began to wonder, "Could *I* be happier as my fullest self?"

Once Anna saw this vision of what life would be like if she could be her whole self at work—but also cultivate a life outside of work—she could not unsee that vision. As one of the few women in the boardroom, she owed it to others to be this fuller version of herself.

So, she wrote her next novel (and the one after that, and the one after that) as Anna Gomez. No one at Leo Burnett even batted an eye. In fact, they embraced her (all of her!) by throwing a party and celebrating with cake—and a press release announcing her true identity to the world.

ARE YOU READY
FOR THIS RIDE?

Hello, fellow oddballs! I'm so glad you are here. Isn't it terrifying to fly your flashy, flamboyant freak flag high atop the Tent of Oddities? Been there, flown that, and can promise: it only gets easier.

Here's the funny thing about being uncomfortable: It's a skill, like any other. The more you do it, the more comfortable you get with being uncomfortable. So, let us see you—the *real* you—because living out loud with no apologies will encourage other people to show up as the real *them*, too.

In other words, I need you to be *you* so that I can be *me*.

As you seek the courage to live fully into this discovery of a new you, consider the following questions:

- Who could you become if you embraced everything that makes you special?
- Can you live more fully into this person by helping others live more fully into the best version of themselves, too?
- What talents come naturally to you (even though others may think they are magical) that you have dismissed as not being special?

Letting Go of Your Demons

★

Before you can fully embrace this new you and venture further on your exciting new path, you have to let go of any demons haunting you—even those you may have concealed from yourself. You'll come face-to-face with all of them in the Haunted House, but don't shrink away in fright: opportunity lies within, amid the fears and forebodings. Put on your bravest face, creep through the darkness, and confront the ghosts lurking there so you can move forward with understanding, forgiveness, and love.

Facing the Past

Chris Plough was racing across the Gobi Desert in a secondhand ambulance when the engine blew out, just two hundred miles from the finish line in Ulaanbaatar, Mongolia. When the ambulance broke down, so did Chris.

"I was thirty-three, and I had it all: the seven-figure business, the house, the car, the toys. And it didn't matter," he recollects. "I told everybody I was happy, but I wasn't."

Chris had started out in wonder, but he couldn't outrun the demons that kept him trapped in his personal hell. Just three years earlier, he had lost both of his parents in a murder-suicide. Unable to process this horrific tragedy, he balled it up and swallowed it down, focusing instead on growing his business, amassing more wealth, and buying more toys. Then the economy tanked.

"My customers stopped paying, and I went bankrupt. I was going further and further into debt just to make payroll," he says. "My friends didn't know what was going on, because my ego wouldn't allow me to tell anyone that I was failing."

So, when a friend proposed racing across Europe and Asia in a second-hand ambulance, Chris couldn't say no. It was an opportunity to keep running, to fill the void with another accolade. He was determined to prove his worth to the world—and to himself.

But the adventure he got was not the one he expected. Forty days later, after nine thousand miles of broken brakes, broken headlights, broken doors, and now a broken engine, Chris was forced to stop running. He had to come to terms with the fact that he was going to fail—again. And this time everyone would know.

"I just wept," he recalls. "I looked out into the desert, and it reminded me of New Mexico, the last place I lived with my parents." Finally ready to process what had happened, he took a framed picture of his parents given to him by his sister and buried it in a small grave in the desert. For the first time, he allowed himself to grieve.

"I realized just how unhappy I'd been for so long," he explains. Driven by denial and fear and the trappings of success, Chris had found only isolation and depression. He was carrying around the heavy weight of never being good enough or worthy enough for his deceased father. "I sought more recognition, more money, more things, more awards, trying to fill that hole," he admits now, "and all it did was get emptier and emptier."

Chris returned to the United States knowing that he needed to make some fundamental changes. So, he did what any type A entrepreneur would do. He recreated the paradigm that had led to his success in the business world. "I decided I'd one-hundred-twenty-hours-a-week this problem," he jokes. "I'd out-meditate everyone else and put the pedal to the medal to advance toward enlightenment and fulfillment." It didn't work.

So Chris began a different type of adventure. He stopped letting his demons dictate his self-worth, and chose something much simpler instead: awareness.

"I spent time thinking about what I've done in my life where I have felt fulfilled and happy," he reveals. "And that began to shift my actions so I was doing more of the things that filled me up, and fewer things that emptied me out." Having finally faced his past, he was free to embrace his future.

Rather than focusing on money or even building a bigger, better business, Chris focused on and invested deeply in relationships, living life more fully, and understanding himself. He started taking responsibility for how he showed up in the world, consciously and unconsciously. As a side effect of this process, his business hit eight figures for the first time—all because he started accepting himself as he was: a work in progress.

Choose Yourself

Why do we spend so much time running from our inner darkness and trying to please other people as though they can give us whatever we've been missing? Do we think that emptiness within will be automatically filled if we just get that next raise, that next promotion, that next spanking-new fancy whoozit or whatsit? Do we hope that then those people will finally see us and love us?

Here's the hard truth: they won't.

It's not that most people are mean-spirited or actively looking to harm you. They just aren't paying attention to you. In fact, most of us are so worried about what everyone else thinks about *us*, we don't have time to think about *anyone else* at all. As the old saying goes, you'd worry much less about what other people think of you if you realized how seldom they do.

Everyone has this void, this empty space, this wrong that needs righting. How do I know? Because we all went to middle school, and no one escapes middle school unscathed. Likewise, no one else is ever going to fill that void you have carved out, held close, and nurtured all these years. It's got to be you.

You created the void within you, even if the trauma was provoked by someone else. You've pointed your finger and asserted your claims over the years with every bit of confirmation bias you could muster. But in truth, it was you who emboldened your demons—just like I empowered mine. If we are being honest with ourselves, we know that other people have no way to earn this power over us unless we let them. Their actions didn't build this void; our interpretation of their actions did.

But if we each made our own void, if we nurtured it and protected it and clung to it with every bit of our identity as we struggled toward success, how do we fix it? The bad news is, your personal house of horrors is your own creation. The good news is, you have access to the architectural plans. You know where every screw and bolt can be found. As you look toward your *next* success, you can begin to dismantle this artificial void, if you so choose.

You must be ready, though, to take two very important steps. First, you must realize that you've imprisoned yourself in this struggle. Second, you must decide that it is finally time to do something about it.

Chris didn't realize the darkness that had grown within him until he was on his knees, sobbing in the desert. But once he saw what was happening, he had to make a decision. Would he continue to pursue more, more, more—striving to earn the unattainable love of someone who was now gone? Or would he acknowledge that he was the only one who could decide he was worthy and restore his wholeness?

Deep into the lonely miles in the desert, Chris refused to fight this war against himself any further, and that changed everything. He chose to let go of his demons, and in doing so was able to finally choose himself.

It is far easier to point fingers, pass the blame, and shirk responsibility than it is to face the truth, do the hard yards, and make the unsexy changes so we can live a more fulfilling life. Perhaps you're afraid to let people down. Perhaps you fear that on your own, you'll be less successful in your new pursuits. Perhaps you dread that crisis of identity when you are no longer the person whom others knew before.

But letting go of everyone else's expectations and yardsticks—whether real or just perceived—will allow you to put yourself, and what matters to you, first. Then you can start moving forward out of the darkness, and perhaps even learn to forgive.

Choose Forgiveness

Every sad-sack romantic saga I Oreo-sleeved my way through as a teenager included the whirlwind of falling in love, the heartbreak of being dumped, and the emotional release of telling off the jerk before falling into the arms of The One. The happy-ending narrative we hear over and over informs us that the cure for any devastating emotional upheaval is the magical moment when you look someone in the eye, lay out your case, and finally get closure.

Naturally, then, we have spent a lifetime pursuing this moment when the angels sing "Hallelujah!" in perfect, high-pitched harmony—first in friendships and romance, and later in business relationships. We've come to believe that the only way to reach peace and file away our experience for posterity is to relitigate the entire drama with the person who caused the harm in the first place, and then to either ask for or award final forgiveness. So we act in a certain prescribed way, hoping to extract the right response that will get us to the place where we emotionally need to be. Each time, we're left frustrated, without answers, and without that mythical closure.

And that doesn't even take into consideration cases like Chris and his father, for whom it was too late to have the conversation at all. But it's possible, as Chris learned, to get to a place of healing even without that particular type of closure.

According to Dr. John Sharp, author of *The Insight Cure*—which reveals how our personal narrative (the story we tell our unconscious about ourselves) affects our decisions, our life, and our happiness—closure isn't necessary to reach forgiveness. When I pressed Dr. Sharp about my endless need for closure, he said, "You know, Laura, forgiveness doesn't have to be couples therapy."

Mind. Blown.

What if, even without the cooperation of that other person, we could simply choose to move on?

Kyle Sanders has taken this one step further. In his career as a wealth advisor, he works with families to identify the values that will shape their financial and philanthropic legacies. Doing so effectively and with integrity meant he, too, needed to identify the values he holds dear. As an entrepreneur, endurance athlete, husband, and father, he chose the following: discipline, agency, and forgiveness.

The first two values might seem obvious—discipline is the hallmark of any endurance athlete, and agency is a trait found in every entrepreneur. But the third, forgiveness, grew out of a spontaneous moment of healing in Kyle's own life: holding the hand of a kindly stranger in a church service when he was in eighth grade, telling her about how his grandfather's murder had shaped his childhood. Through this experience, Kyle came to understand what would become the foundation for the rest of his life: none of us deserve to be defined by the worst thing we've ever done. No matter how egregious the act, it's merely *part* of our story. This understanding set Kyle free from a burden that otherwise would have drowned him.

If Kyle had been unable to find this forgiveness inside himself, his life would look much different today. "I let go of the hate and the anger," he says, "and through that I was able to hold on to something else: love and peace." As Kyle realized, you can't make peace with yourself if you won't offer it to someone else.

This quest for a type of closure that comes from within, not from without, set him on a path of understanding what matters to him and living into those values every day, on purpose and with intention. These days, in his podcast *Legacy on Purpose*, Kyle interviews other athletes, entrepreneurs, and thought leaders about how they manifest their values in their own daily lives. What he has found further underscores the lesson he learned so long ago: choosing forgiveness is a watershed moment that releases you from every open tab, hanging chad, or banging screen door that has left you in limbo for days, weeks, months, years, even decades.

As you step through the gateway to this next stage of your life, it's best to leave behind the ghosts of your past. Forgive, let go, and move on from that endless, unfulfilling wait, from that slow leak of valuable energy as you anticipate someone else's reaction that may never arrive. Forgiveness is the only way to escape the hell of constantly looping back to the actions and thoughts of other people, so you can fully embrace the wonder of what comes next.

Choose Love

Dr. Martin Luther King Jr. said, "Darkness cannot drive out darkness; only light can do that. Hate cannot drive out hate; only love can do that." So why do we traffic in darkness, allowing the hate to swallow us whole, instead of seeking a better path forward?

Now, don't worry. This isn't going to be some toxic positivity screed that tells you to "just be happy," as if that's the secret to finding success as you confront your next Wonderhell. Forcing yourself to be happy just to conform with societal expectations is pointless. Breaking a cycle of festering negativity shackled to your ankles by someone else, however, is advantageous. The former causes *more* pain; the latter releases it.

Don't get me wrong—I'm all for the negative emotions that accompany us into Wonderhell. Uncertainty, fear, pressure, and anxiety can be useful (as you'll see in the next part of this book, which explores Doubtsville) in telling us we are on the right track, and in motivating us to cross the finish line of our next great success.

What's more, experiencing negative emotions can make us feel happier, when those negative emotions are the ones we actively and intentionally want to be feeling in that moment.[1] Ugly-crying at funerals, for example, can be cathartic.

You simply can't feel emotions on one end of the spectrum without experiencing the other. It's why the hell grows, every time, in relation to the wonder. Your ability to feel the deepest pain allows you to expand your range into the deepest joy. So, yeah, feeling that pain is good for you.

Knowing that it can open the door to joy—should you choose it—is good for you, too. Exploring that darkness is a step toward understanding the full complexity of your emotional range. In her book *Emotional Agility*, Dr. Susan David reminds us that every feeling we experience can be interpreted in a multitude of ways.

---

1 Maya Tamir, PhD, et al., "The Secret to Happiness: Feeling Good or Feeling Right?," *Journal of Experimental Psychology: General*, August 2017.

If you are feeling embarrassed, that might be related to deeper feelings of self-consciousness, isolation, loneliness, inferiority, guilt, shame, or confusion.

If you are feeling angry, you might be frustrated, grumpy, annoyed, defensive, irritated, disgusted, offended, or spiteful.

If you are feeling anxious, that could come from fear, confusion, stress, vulnerability, skepticism, worry, caution, or nervousness.

Susan's advice? If you are experiencing a strong emotion, take a moment to consider what to call it. "But don't stop there," she suggests. "Once you've identified it, try to come up with two more words that describe how you are feeling. You might be surprised at the breadth of your emotions—or at how you've unearthed a deeper emotion buried beneath the more obvious one."

Identifying our emotional reactions can help us untangle the struggles that persist in the dark corners of our consciousness. We talk to ourselves all day, every day, narrating our own story, and we become the words we speak. So when we choose to focus our self-talk on the negative, the negative is what we get. The same goes for focusing on the positive.

Every time you choose love, you allow yourself the grace to be who you are, warts and all.

Perhaps that's enough to convince you not only to identify your emotions carefully and choose your focus wisely, but also to adjust their strength and volume according to what's actually happening. If not, consider this: pessimists die, on average, two years earlier than optimists.[2] So every time you choose the positive over the negative, you are not only improving your luck (as the Fortune Teller foretold) and revealing the new you (the one who appeared in the Imaginarium)—but you are also extending your life.

Pausing now and again on your road through each Wonderhell will let you assign the true emotion to how you are feeling—and will ensure it is the appropriate one for that moment. These pauses will allow you to choose love, even if that means actively choosing to walk away.

---

2 Toshihiko Maruto, MD, et al., "Optimists vs Pessimists: Survival Rate Among Medical Patients Over a 30-Year Period," *Mayo Clinic Proceedings*, 2000.

Walking Away from "Not Yet"

Jill Sherer Murray had a choice to make about Hector. She had spent twelve years waiting to talk about next steps, waiting to live together, waiting to get married. And she had spent twelve years hearing Hector say, "Not yet."

One day, a realtor friend told Jill about a newly available apartment. Jill mentioned it to Hector, expecting to get the usual "Not yet," but to her surprise, he agreed to go see it. At the appointed hour, Jill was there. The realtor was there. But Hector was not. The minutes ticked by until he finally called and asked to reschedule for later in the day—when Hector was a no-show once again.

"It was the lowest moment of my life—but also a pivotal one," Jill says now. "In that moment I decided, after twelve years, it was time to let go. I had to let go of Hector and the idea of marrying him and, at age forty-one, maybe the idea of marrying anyone." And she had to imagine who she could be without all of these things.

Jill chose herself, and in doing so, she also chose forgiveness and love. Letting go of Hector, along with the hopes and dreams she had attached to him, meant she had to let go of some things she'd held on to for far too long: taking things personally, yielding to what other people thought, trying to be something she was not, needing to be perfect—and listening to people in her life when they repeatedly told her, "Not yet."

Jill realized, as she tells us in her book *Big Wild Love: The Unstoppable Power of Letting Go*, that she was the sum total of everything that had come before her and had been poured into her. You and I are no different. We carry injury and trauma (as well as hopes and dreams) from our parents, grandparents, and other people in our lives, like rocks piled one after one into a backpack strapped to our shoulders. Some of those people may have bullied, tortured, or gaslit us into feeling a certain way about ourselves, which leaves that backpack heavier and heavier. But often this has way more to do with them and their pain than with us. Hurt people hurt people. But as Jill points out, *you* get to decide what to do with that stuff.

Jill decided to make it part of her story. The painful things no longer weigh her down; they make her stronger. But that doesn't mean choosing to let go was the easy way out.

"There were days when I wanted to go back to bed," she admits. "But there were days where I didn't." Clinging to her self-esteem issues, and staying in a relationship that wasn't serving her needs, came at a price: she was allowing her demons to control her rather than living fully into her life. Now, she no longer expects to conquer all her issues or pressures herself to be perfect all the time. She asks herself, *Are my feelings getting in the way of living?*

When the answer is no, she just makes the feelings part of who she is.

When the answer is yes, she lets them go. "Letting go can make you unstoppable," Jill reports.

Within a year of leaving Hector and "Not yet," Jill found the love of her life, to whom she is happily married today. And she discovered the best part about letting go: without all the bad stuff haunting her, she found plenty of room in her heart for joy, courage, and adventure.

ARE YOU READY
FOR THIS RIDE?

As you journey through Wonderhell, you may be tempted to squander your energy in pursuing the love, respect, and admiration of others—and the Haunted House is a perfect opportunity to expel those demons. Do those people or their opinions truly matter in your life? As you reach for your next success, does seeking approval or requiring forgiveness add depth to your story, or does it just weigh you down?

When you turn away from the ghosts in your path—the judgments, assessments, opinions, and unfinished business—you can choose yourself, choose love, choose this moment.

As you decide to unburden yourself from your demons, consider the following questions:

- What expectations have you been carrying around, and are they serving you?

- Have any of the grudges that you have gathered along the way incentivized you to become stronger, faster, better—or are they closing off your access to hope, joy, and adventure?
- Who are you prioritizing today, and why isn't it you?

TUNNEL OF **LOVE** THIS WAY

Going Farther
Together

THE **SCRAMBLER**

Finding Your
Own Way

THE **FERRIS WHEEL**

Gaining Perspective
on Other People

THE TRAPEZE

Flying without
a Net

THE **ROLLER COASTER**

Managing
Uncertainty

DOUBTSVILLE

YOU ARE HERE

DOUBTSVILLE

RENEGOTIATE
YOUR RESPONSE

You did it! You embraced your ambition and envisioned something you didn't think was possible: a bigger and better you.

But wait . . . now what?!

A tsunami of emotions is roaring toward you, and they aren't all good. Some of them feel downright horrible. You are filled with dread, discomfort, and doubt. Not only that, but you have no idea where to go, how to be, or even who to be.

Chaos rises from within and threatens to throw you off track:

Why does my next move still feel so uncertain, even after my past success?

What if I fail this time?

Am I ready to move forward, or is something holding me back?

Your jumbled-up emotions are screaming at you to stop, do an about-face, and hightail it to safety. But what if these emotions are merely a sign that you're on the right track? What if the uneasiness you feel is your pathway to growth?

If you haven't realized it by now, you're in Doubtsville.

Managing Uncertainty

★

Take a seat on the Roller Coaster! It's going to be a wild and bumpy trip. You will be excited, you will be uncertain, you will be scared . . . but you will figure it out anyway. Choose your seatmate wisely and hold on tight as you rev up the incline. *Tick, tick, tick!* Up you go, anticipating the thrilling, terrifying acceleration awaiting you just over the peak. You're about to discover how to get comfortable being uncomfortable. By the time you reach the highest elevation, you'll be ready to let go and enjoy the ride.

Showing Up, Even When It's Uncomfortable

Kara Goldin had a problem. Actually, she had several problems: post-baby weight gain, adult-onset acne, and inescapable exhaustion. So, she did what many of us would do to cut calories and fight sleep: she pounded caffeinated diet soda, often ten to twelve cans per day. But the more she drank, the worse she felt.

It couldn't be the sodas. She needed the caffeine to wake her up. And the label said ZERO CALORIES, so that wasn't why she was gaining weight. Right? (Wrong.) Kara sought help from her doctors, but she was dismissed again and again: *It's aging! It's hormones! It's normal!* But to Kara, it felt anything but normal.

One day Kara glimpsed the long list of unpronounceable ingredients and had a startling realization. "I was paying more attention to the liquid

I was putting into my car than the liquid I was putting into my body," she remembers. "I knew I had to drink more water—but I hated water."

Surely there must be a healthy flavored water I can buy instead of my favorite diet soda, she thought. *Right?* (Wrong again.) Each drink she found had more unpronounceable ingredients than the last. If Kara wanted this magical product, she was going to have to make it herself. And so for months, Kara sliced up fruit and steeped it into her water, until finally, she got a call from her doctor with an answer—just not to the question she originally asked.

That afternoon, she broke the double-edged news to her husband: she was three months pregnant with their fourth child (all under age six!), and she'd decided to start a beverage company that would change the entire industry.

"I told Theo that we had six months to get the business going until—surprise!—baby number four was born," she recalls. "He walked out of the room, and I wasn't sure if he was coming back."

But he did come back, and it was Theo who, after many failed attempts, finally figured out how to make the drink shelf-stable. Success at last!

But if Kara and Theo thought building the product was a challenge, they had no idea how much harder it would be to launch Hint Water and successfully scale it up to a $150 million beverage company. The road ahead, through each Wonderhell, was paved with doubt.

Kara and Theo asked their local Whole Foods to stock Hint, and then stood by it even when the product experienced some early issues. When mold became a problem, Theo opened a bottle and drank the whole thing while the store manager watched, to prove it was still healthy. When Starbucks decided to stop carrying Hint, Kara went to work finding new distributors. When the pandemic hit, Kara took over a distribution route herself, delivering Hint to retail outlets in the San Francisco Bay Area. Throughout development and at each crisis point, the future was uncertain. But Kara chose to show up, even when she could hardly see a clear path forward.

Here's what's clever about showing up hard when things get hard: it gives you knowledge, it gives you data, and it gives you options. "You've got to have options," Kara explains. "When you feel like someone has you by the throat, that's a huge indicator that you don't have enough choices." Believe it or not, that hand on your throat might be the wake-up call you've been waiting for.

When you're facing uncertainty, exploring all possible avenues really is essential. As Kara understood, seeing for yourself the potential outcomes requires getting a lay of the land and feeling things out—on the ground, in the trenches, experiencing the good, the bad, and the ugly. Just ask the manager at a Target in San Francisco, who was so shocked and impressed to discover that the new delivery person stocking his shelves with Hint Water was the founder and CEO herself, that he offered even more display space—and asked for her autograph on a bottle.

To Kara, anything was possible as long as she was willing to get uncomfortable—and ignore the voice in her head telling her it couldn't be done.

Impeach the Governor

Cars once were built standard with an electronic device called a governor that would limit the top speed of the vehicle. No matter how much the motorist floored the gas pedal, the governor prevented the car from exceeding the predetermined and relatively safe maximum of 100 mph. Even though engines were built to withstand higher speeds, the governor was there to stop the driver from doing something stupid and burning the motor out.

There is a voice in your brain that acts like a governor, too. It stops you from burning yourself out, screaming at you to cease anything that might be scary, foreign, or uncertain.

Danger! You've never done this before! it cries, pumping you full of fear and stress.

Halt! You don't know enough! it cautions, cleaving open your doubt and insecurity.

No! You might embarrass yourself! it nags, slowing you down and siphoning off your spirit of adventure.

But what if you reprogrammed that voice so it no longer cautioned you against doing something untried and experimental? Instead of the governor's warning, what if you heard the rousing call of a cheerleader, applauding you for trying something new and original?

Woohoo! You've never done this before! replaces the shadowy omen of your fear with a celebration of your bravery.

Keep going! You don't know enough! replaces finite judgment with a green light to learn and grow.

Yes! You might embarrass yourself! replaces an alarm bell indicating that you will be ridiculed with a reminder that failure need not define you in the future, any more than success has defined you in the past.

In other words, you could accept your governor's reflection of you as an impostor and just stop trying. You could heed your governor's warning of doom and gloom, play it safe, and avoid venturing too much. Or you could decide your governor is a pervasive, loud-mouthed weenie.

The only way to embrace your true potential is to get comfortable pushing the limits and forging ahead. To figure out you who you are—and who you want to be next—you'll need to retrofit your brain to perceive this governor not as a limitation, but as an invitation to push beyond what you previously thought possible.

Listen between the lines, and you may find that voice is actually insisting that you've exhausted what your engine can do at this speed—and urging you to go boldly into the vast unknown. I don't want you to silence it. I want you to increase its volume and be excited by it. That voice isn't instructing you to downshift; it's welcoming you to your newfound potential and inviting you to upshift into another gear. It's not your governor; it's your cheering section.

Your governor is the hell. Your cheering section is the wonder. And it's ready to show you everything you could ever be, if you just let it convince you that you are worthy of that dream.

The first step is taking action.

Just Take Action

Have you ever been faced with so much doubt and indecision that you felt positively paralyzed by it? What did you do? How did you decide? Was it the right or wrong decision in the end? And how do you really know, anyway?

Life doesn't give us a control group and an experimental group, so you can simulate the outcomes stemming from one set of choices versus another. You just have to make the best decision you can with the fullest data set available to you—bearing in mind that you will never, in fact, have a completely full set of data. Maybe you don't remember it quite this way, but getting to your initial success probably—just like now—involved winging it sometimes.

So, when you don't have all the information, what do you do? How do you make that first, catalyzing decision to get past the tsunami of doubt?

You simply do *something*. Anything, in fact.

When struggling to make big life choices—leaving a job, ending a relationship, seeking more education, quitting smoking—studies show people who flip a coin and "go for it" regardless of the outcome are more satisfied with their decisions and much happier six months later than those whose coin toss instructed them to maintain the status quo.[1] Action beats stagnation. When you're unsure about *what* to do, you'll be happiest if you just choose *something* to do.

For me, action isn't typically an issue. When I'm in a groove, I'm golden. But when some new obstacle drops into my path—when I travel, when I have a big deadline, when a client changes their mind mid-project (or when there is, say, a global pandemic)—I lose my way. Unhealthy eating, sickness, frustration, and injury tend to lay me low. And when I stray from the path, I end up practically face down in the gutter.

The best antidote to inaction is action. So, how do we motivate ourselves to start again?

We don't.

I may be considered a motivational speaker, but I don't put much stock in motivation. As for dipping into that mystical well of enthusiasm, searching for the inner drive to do that hard task, write that difficult email, run that painful mile—no, thanks! It's too easy to avoid that task, make excuses not to write that email, break a promise with myself to run that mile. But I would never,

---

1 Steven D. Levitt, "Heads or Tails: The Impact of a Coin Toss on Major Life Decisions and Subsequent Happiness," *Review of Economic Studies*, May 2020.

ever break a promise to you. Motivation won't get me out of bed at 5 a.m. to run alone, but if I'm meeting you, bet your bottom dollar I'll be there with bells on.

That's why the road to action is not through motivation but through accountability.

Being accountable to others will get you back on track when everything in your core yearns to slather itself in indecision, uncertainty, or malaise. When you're facing something formidable, accountability focuses you on the here-and-now activity, not the unknown result. So, look around, figure out the First Action to take, and ask a friend to join you.

The First Action doesn't need to be the Perfect Action. Simply putting one foot in front of the other gives you a feeling of power, control, and choice. It starts you, however gradually, on the road to longer-term satisfaction and happiness. Course correction can come later.

And remember, choosing to be still for a time while you gather more information counts as action, too, as long as it's an intentional choice (and includes a time limit). Whatever step you choose to take—even if you're not quite sure which direction you're heading—you are answering the external uncertainty of the moment with the certainty of action.

We See You, We Feel You, We Are You

In August 2020, Michelle Obama revealed that she had been suffering from low-grade depression.

My response? *I see you. I feel you. I am you.*

I was struck by the fact that someone like her, with access to every possible resource in the world, was feeling just like me. So I bit the bullet and posted about it on social media. My surprise about Mrs. Obama was nothing compared to how gobsmacked I was when a hundred other people responded who finally felt that they, too, could admit to feeling lower than ever before.

We see you. We feel you. We are you.

In 2020, the Centers for Disease Control and Prevention confirmed the pervasiveness of these feelings. One in three Americans reported symptoms of depression or anxiety, more than three times the rate from a similar survey conducted in early 2019.[2] Given the effect of the coronavirus pandemic on our careers, our bank accounts, our families, and our friends—plus the political upheaval in advance of the 2020 elections, and the racial reckoning afoot—emotions were bursting into uncharted territory for all of us.

Uncertainty is part and parcel of Wonderhell.˙

One of the hardest parts of reaching new heights is the realization that whatever got you here only gets you into starting position for your newly expanded potential; it's not enough to get you across the finish line. You've perfected a skill, a brand, a message, a work ethic, an outlook. And it has paid dividends in opportunities and success. But each new level brings a new devil.

And that devil can feel like depression when it takes over.

If you have clinical depression or are struggling with anxiety, and you are attempting to go it alone, I urge you to seek medical attention. There is great help out there, and you deserve to have it. However, if instead you are experiencing something that feels temporary, unusual, and circumstance-driven, let's unpack what might be happening in your mind.

Depicting mental health issues like depression or anxiety as simply chemical imbalances doesn't fully express their complexity. Rather than just a function of your brain having too much or too little of certain chemicals, depression and anxiety can be a result of faulty mood regulation, the stresses that life brings, certain medications or their underlying medical problems, or simply the genes you inherited.[3] And when several of these forces interact, your mental health is often the first casualty.

Have the demands of your new Wonderhell shifted into uncharted territory? Has your schedule changed? Have you ended a relationship? Are you doing things you've never done before? Are you being asked to manage a larger team? Are the metrics, goals, and levels bigger than ever? For some

2 The Centers for Disease Control and Prevention performs a "Household Pulse Survey" at random seven-day intervals, the data from which may be found at www.cdc.gov/nchs/covid19/pulse/mental-health.htm.
3 "What Causes Depression?," *Harvard Health Publishing*, January 10, 2022, https://www.health.harvard.edu/mind-and-mood/what-causes-depression.

one accustomed to always being on top of things, these expectations might be a daunting, even damaging burden.

Now let's take a look at any recent physical changes. Are you sleeping enough? Are you eating well? Are you hydrated? Are you moving your body? Are you drinking too much caffeine, alcohol, or diet soda? Each of these factors could create a disruption in your brain chemistry by switching up the chemicals like dopamine, endorphins, oxytocin, and serotonin that your brain uses to regulate itself.

So, when life gets chaotic, your routine gets disrupted, and a downward spiral begins, check in with yourself—mind, body, and soul. And take comfort (as I did) in knowing that just about everyone has, at some point, felt the way you feel now. You are not alone. Uncertainty is unsettling. We feel you, we see you, we are you.

And if certain things just aren't working for you right now, fall back on what *does* work for you—what is within your span of control.

Focusing on Your Span of Control

Carey Lohrenz knows a thing or two about uncertainty. After all, she was one of the first female F-14 Tomcat fighter pilots in the US Navy, and one of the few people on the planet brave enough (or crazy enough) to land that $45 million piece of equipment on a postage stamp of an aircraft carrier rollicking in forty-foot ocean swells.

When Carey landed her plane, she would hit the deck going 145 knots (nearly 170 miles per hour). The arresting hook on her Tomcat would snag a wire, and she would slam both throttles to full military power and click her speed brakes. If all worked well, her body would jerk forward with such force that her arms and legs felt as though they might separate from her body. She would go from more than twice the speed of the average roller coaster to a full stop in just 1.2 seconds.

It was a high-pressure situation with no room for doubt, especially the first time you glimpse the landing strip at the back end of that carrier. "You'll find your humility—or your personal Jesus, in whatever form that may be," Carey says. "Now imagine that same scenario *at night,* when you are a thousand miles away from shore and you cannot control the environment—the gusty winds, the overpowering darkness, the crashing waves, the moving target."

To handle this vomit-inducing stress, Carey focused on what she calls her "span of control." In that moment, so many things were outside of her control: the weather, the ship, the tasking, the communication system, the aircraft systems, and her teammates' reactions to stress, just to name a few. So, she chose to concentrate on the three most critical things: meatball, line-up, and angle of attack.

The *meatball* is the light that indicates the optimal glide path. The *line-up* is the centerline of the aircraft carrier's landing area. The *angle of attack* refers to the position of the wings relative to the wind. Each of these factors changes continuously, and for the landing to happen safely, everything has to be perfect. It's that simple, but also that complex. Meatball, line-up, angle of attack—just three things within the pilot's span of control. In the mere seconds it takes to execute the landing, everything else falls away.

Carey believes so deeply in this approach that she published a best-selling book called *Span of Control* in 2021 and sports an *SoC* tattoo on the inside of her right wrist as a reminder. You see, Carey learned the hard way that she could use this same technique to manage uncertainty in her civilian life: while raising a family, caring for dying parents, and pandemic-pivoting a career from speaking on stages at events to mastering audiovisual technology for remote client engagements.

"When you have four little kids, own a business, and make everyone else a priority, there is no end point," Carey explains about the moment her health began to fail her. "I loved my life, my kids, my husband—and I was running on fumes."

Her heart began racing erratically, and Carey had several episodes of feeling suddenly, inexplicably as though she might pass out. For someone who had tested every bit of her strength, commitment, and stamina many times over—someone who had won the Head of the Charles as a Division I collegiate rower and completed arduous pre-Olympic training; endured sixteen weeks of grueling physical, psychological, and academic training during Aviation Officer Candidate School; and pulled six to eight G-Forces as a fighter pilot—this reaction to stress and uncertainty was unsettling. Carey needed to renegotiate her response.

So, she went back to basics and picked her three highest priorities, labeled on sticky-notes attached to her computer—throughout the ups and downs of the pandemic, for example, it was *family, finances,* and *fitness*. She says no to anything that doesn't contribute to her three critical imperatives. She focuses on what matters, where she can have an impact, and how best to get things done.

Simply put, she focuses on what is within her span of control.

ARE YOU READY FOR THIS RIDE?

Life is always up and up, better and better . . . until it's not. Enter the Roller Coaster, with steep climbs and sudden drops and who-knows-what's-next! One thing is certain: nothing is ever certain. Although there's no way to consider every possible contingency, you've got control over one choice: figure out how you'll show up when things go sideways.

Showing up prepared to act, even when the best action is unclear, deepens your understanding of the problem and reveals the solutions that are in your span of control. Just taking that first brave step lets everyone know you are in this no matter what—ready to transform the hell of uncertainty to the wonder of opportunity.

As you stare out at the changing horizon with its impossible rises and invisible falls, preparing to solve this new level's new devil, consider the following questions:

- How has your *It's always been done this way!* mindset obstructed your ability to innovate and iterate a new solution?
- What action can you take—today! right now!—to move forward and build momentum for what lies ahead?
- What is in your span of control, and what needs to fall out of focus so you can manage this uncertainty?

Flying without a Net

★

Look at you, flying through the air on the Trapeze! Just don't look down or you'll discover that there is no safety net—and there never was. Only by climbing high enough, swinging above your wildest dreams, will you realize there's no perfect way to be, perfect time to start, or perfect decision to make. That safety net you imagined was only an illusion. Higher and higher you go, making it up as you go along—just like the rest of us.

Not Perfect, Just Perfectly You

Jen Welter developed a bit of a reputation for never backing down on the rugby pitch. When she accidentally broke her opponent's leg after a legal tackle, that reputation became legend. Every team in professional women's football was looking at "Little Bone Breaker" Welter, which was unusual for a person standing only five feet, two inches tall.

Her career would eventually include four world championships, two gold medals, and eight all-star selections. She was inducted into the first class of the Women's Football Hall of Fame in 2018. But her exploits in women's football aren't what cemented Jen's place in history—nor would performing on the gridiron be the last time she had to fly without a net.

Jen was the first woman to play running back in a men's professional football league, the Texas Revolution, an arena football team. "When I went into the men's game, I was like, 'Man, you're gonna have to cut me or kill me, because I'm not quitting,'" she remembers telling her coach. She was glad to be the first, but dead set on not being the last. No way was she going to give them a reason to close the door on the next woman. She refused to participate in a narrative that went *Well, we had a girl once, but . . .*

She wanted to be a real player, not some spectacle or publicity stunt, and that meant stepping up to every fresh challenge the game put in her way. She wasn't looking for perfection—just looking to perfect her own personal game. At every turn, she prepared more, watched more tape, built more muscle. A true pioneer, she had no one to compete against; it was Jen versus Jen on the road to personal greatness, with no road map to follow.

Because her situation was unique—she didn't have size on her side—Jen had to break down the plays into microsteps to gain an understanding of the science of torque, the physics of balance, and the psychology of the game. In time, without realizing it, she had custom-made herself into a great coach.

She landed a spot as the first female coach in men's professional football, contributing to the Revolution's highly successful season. Then, in 2015, she became the linebackers coach for the Arizona Cardinals—the first female coach in the NFL.

Once again, there was no net, no narrative to follow.

Jen didn't want to be a woman in a man's world. "I wanted to be the best me I could be in a world that *happened* to be all men but didn't *have* to be all men," she explains. She continued to paint her fingernails, for example, because she wanted little girls to see that you could be feminine and still be tough. But coaching in a whole new way—a perfectly Jen way—entailed far more than nail polish.

"There's a lot of yelling in football," she says. But at five foot two, if she tried to get all up in a player's face, she wouldn't be toe to toe, but chest to belly button. She couldn't yell loud enough or close enough that players would have to listen. Fundamentally, her coaching was not going to be business as usual.

So she tried the opposite of the usual.

"My philosophy was that if tensions were high, I would be the master of the strong 'pull aside,'" Jen explains. "Anyone can lean in for a whisper." And she made that method work perfectly for her.

And what happened when she pulled players aside and whispered her wisdom? They not only saw her love for them and for the sport; they also saw her being wholly authentic to who she was. They saw that she was not trying to be perfect, but just working every day to be *her* best so they could be *their* best. And they trusted her so much that they would lean in, heed that whisper, and choose to follow up with a question, "Hey, Coach, what else you got?"

All the World Is Improv

Years ago I got some improv training. It wasn't by choice.

In fact, improv comedy probably ranks up there at the very top of the "Things I Hate to Do" list. No shade to those of you who love improv; I'm just a control freak. Quack like a duck? Bark like a dog? End someone else's sentences? Belittle myself for the bemusement of a crowd of random strangers? Hard pass. But as part of my journey to become a better public speaker, I signed up for a weekend of speaker training, and one of the sessions was improv.

Until recently, I would write a script, memorize the script, and cling to that script while onstage, grateful for the assistance and protection offered by the notes clutched in my hand. I feared that if I deviated from that script, even by just one word, I'd spontaneously combust, right there in front of a thousand audience members. I knew I showed promise as a speaker, but the burden of my potential would be alleviated only if I got some help to get me to the next level.

That help came in the form of Mike Ganino, although I didn't appreciate this right away. To my chagrin, his improv training sessions that weekend were not optional. Luckily, the auditorium was giant, and my first thought was, *Phew! I can go hide in the back.* And that's exactly what I did. But in walked Mike, whose joyous appeal for every single one of us to come onstage and form a giant circle around him made me loathe him immediately.

I freaked out (*Ack! I can't hide!*), though I soon discovered that Mike is a lovely human, and we became dear friends. But in the moment, he was taking away my safety net—and that made him my sworn enemy.

In the beginning, Mike made us do all the things you'd expect from improv. Yes, we quacked like ducks, barked like dogs, and ended each other's sentences. It was mortifying. But it also kicked off a profound shift in the way I would begin to show up onstage.

The first thing you learn in improv is never to say *No, but . . .* You always, even if you have no idea where you are going next, must say, *Yes, and . . .* So no matter what happens, you can keep going—even if you mess up onstage in the middle of a keynote speech.

Like when I forget the next line: *Why was I telling you that? Ah, yes, and here's why . . .*

Or when someone's cell phone starts ringing: *Tell them I'm busy, ha! Yes, and as I was saying . . .*

Or when the fire alarm goes off: *Oops, a minor emergency! Yes, and let's move this outside to finish on our feet in the parking lot . . .* (True story, and a guaranteed standing ovation!)

Improv helped me turn the unknown into a playground. Instead of viewing uncertainty as my worst nightmare, I began to look forward to it. I learned to breathe into my experience, keep the stories flowing, jam and ad-lib with other people, and stand strong when panic threatens to take over. No more giving in to my inner *No, but . . .*! Now, I say, *Yes, and . . .* and let go of the fear of falling.

The script you have written for your life—the battle plan for whatever comes our way—is just an illusion. There are no guarantees. And the only way we can truly grow is to remain open to flying without that safety net. Even if we fall, we still have whatever tools and talent got us here, and that will help us get to the next level, too.

Casting aside that script, becoming flexible and open to trying out what frightens you, is essential as you move into your next Wonderhell. Not only that, but it shuts up the negative self-talk that stops you from dreaming even bigger, so your work can speak for itself.

Earn Your Medals in Practice

What do champions think about at the starting line of a race? The answer might surprise you.

In interviews with the planet's most illustrious competitors, from Olympians to Hall of Famers to world record holders, again and again they reveal the secrets of their pregame warm-up, their stretching routine, their idiosyncratic dietary habits. But when asked what performance-enhancing mental practices they employ right before the gun goes off, the answer is almost always the same: "Nothing."

Inconceivable! Yet the through line remains: They've already put in the work. They trust their training. There's nothing left to do but perform.

In the award-winning 2020 documentary series *The Last Dance*, Michael Jordan is asked whether he ever felt fear in high-pressure situations. "Never," he says. "I never feared about my skills, because I put in the work." In his experience, work ethic eliminates fear. If you've done the work—building on your fundamentals, practicing them over and over—what is there to fear? "You know what you're capable of doing," he explains, "and what you're not."

Retired US Navy SEAL Stephen Drum agrees. In addition to being a combat-tested master chief with almost three decades of experience leading teams and executing mission-critical performance strategies, Stephen also co-developed and taught Warrior Toughness training for the US Navy. When it was introduced, the program fundamentally changed the way the Navy prepared young sailors for the acute stress of intense combat operations, when success or failure means life or death. Stephen's expertise comes from handling his own stressful situations, where bullets were literally flying at his head. "I knew I had been trained for any possible scenario, and I knew that my training would see me through."

This sentiment applies to us mere mortals, too. In any high-pressure scenario, the key is to remember you didn't just suddenly come to life in that moment. Instead, that moment is the sum total of everything you have done before it. You trained. You succeeded in smaller arenas. You moved to larger arenas. You messed up, went back to basics, and trained some more. At each level, you found yourself on the brink of spiraling into the perilous abyss of negative self-talk, but you counteracted that by shifting your own narrative.

Don't believe me? I'll prove it to you.

Start by making a list of the things that make you proud: your accomplishments, achievements, awards, conquests. Be bold! I promise I won't tell anyone that you've been bragging. Let it rip! List everything of worth that you've done, both large and small. The cold, hard facts about what you've achieved will bring your work ethic into stark relief. And if work ethic eliminates fear (as world-class athletes and badass Navy SEALs attest), this simple list will shatter that endless, emotional, inner narrative.

Next, list everything that you're afraid might go wrong. Some of your fears will seem silly when written in black and white: You might pass out? Pre-hydrate. You might pee your pants? Don't pre-hydrate too much. When you allow yourself to air your doubts and anxieties, the solutions will seem obvious (and probably easy enough to execute).

Some of your fears will seem overwhelming, of course, but they have solutions, too. You don't know the background of everyone at the presentation? Use the supercomputer in your pocket to do some research. You aren't sure whether your message will go over well? Get feedback from friends who are similar to your target audience. Doing what you can to prepare—again, bearing in mind that you'll never have perfectly complete information—will go a long way toward quieting that inner critic.

Remember, you don't rise to the level of your hopes and dreams; you sink to the level of your preparation. So do the work, and let it remind you of your worth. You may be flying high without a safety net, but your experience and training will support you nonetheless. You've got this. Like every great champion, you've already earned your medals in practice. You just pick them up on game day.

Even Cher Messes Up

Even with all the practice and positive self-talk in the world, being willing to fly without a safety net means you must be willing to mess up sometimes. And that's something we all do—even champions and superstars. I've seen it myself, up close and personal.

A few years ago, my family went on a trip to the American Southwest that started in Sedona, took us through the Grand Canyon, and ended with a flight out of Las Vegas, where we gave our kids the ultimate Vegas show experience: Cher.

She was everything you'd imagine: giant wigs, sky-high heels, and sequined, skin-baring costumes. All ass and sass and, even in her seventies, able to dance me under the table—she was perfect. Yet her perfection didn't stand out for me that night as much as her imperfection.

Have you ever watched someone give a forty-five-minute speech onstage and wondered, *How does she remember all this?* I certainly wondered that when I started speaking at events and worrying about failing miserably—I smoked way too much pot in my youth to rely on my brain alone. Thank goodness, part of that improv nightmare weekend I told you about included another very handy trick, stage blocking.

It goes something like this: If you are talking about the problem while you are on one side of the stage, then you walk over to the other side of the stage to talk about the solution. And when you want to share a detail, you back up to be smaller; then you move forward when sharing the fuller picture. More than a few times now, when I've forgotten what comes next in my speech, I've stopped to think: *I'm over here talking about the problem, which means I need to go over there next, which means . . . Ah yes, it's time for me to say the line about the solution!*

You can imagine how comforting it is, then, to see an old pro like Cher (who also probably smoked a lot of pot in her youth) do this exact same thing. And you'd think her shows would all go off without a hitch by now, but take heart, dear ones, even Cher messes up.

Here's how it went down: In between numbers, Cher paused the music and told a long, rambling, hilarious story, taking us through about six dozen agony and ecstasy moments. At one point, the story got away from her, and she suddenly stopped mid-yarn and stared blankly at the crowd.

"Wait, I think I forgot a part of the story," she chuckled. "Let's see, I'm over here *[points to the part of the stage where she's standing]* and I gotta go over there *[points to the other side of the stage, and then strolls across it and points to where she is now standing]* and this is the bad place, so I gotta tell you the bad part of the story."

At that point I, for one, didn't even care about the story. I was completely transfixed by the buffoonery of it all.

"Oh yeah, that's right," Cher continued, perking up. "So, Jack Nicholson tried to kick me out of *The Witches of Eastwick* because he said I was too old and not sexy . . . And now I gotta go back over there *[points back to where she just was]* because that's the good place, where I can tell you the good part of the story." And she silently walked back across the stage, with all the dramatic pause in the world, and declared, "For that role, I won an Academy Award." And then she curtsied to the uproarious applause, and totally owned it.

Cher has been performing her entire life. At every step and for every stage, including that one in Vegas, she has been a pro. But even *she* messes up! And here's the best part: when I later wrote about this in my newsletter, half a dozen readers reached out to share that they, too, saw her do exactly the same thing when they saw her show on other nights.

At some point, Cher must have truly made this mistake. Yet instead of wavering in doubt, she realized that imperfection was actually more charming, more engaging, more riotously lovable than perfection. So now, the bit she learned while flailing through the air in search of that nonexistent safety net has become a permanent part of her act.

Or maybe it was sheer coincidence. I'll never know. What matters, though, is that she felt comfortable enough to be imperfect, and her comfort level gave her unlimited freedom to explore and improve.

The upshot: Imperfection isn't a sign of weakness. It's a sign of strength.

Hello Darkness, We're Old Friends

Sanford (Sandy) Greenberg was leading a charmed life in New York City. He excelled as a student at Columbia University, taking important classes from important professors such as Richard Neustadt (political science), Margaret Mead (anthropology), and Leon Lederman (physics). He had been accepted into the prestigious White House Fellows program during the Johnson administration. He was madly in love with his girlfriend, Sue, whom he'd first laid eyes upon in Buffalo in sixth grade. And he had a stellar inner circle of talented friends, including his college roommate, Art Garfunkel.

As freshmen at Columbia, Sandy and Art made a pact: if either of them ever saw the other in trouble, he would come to his friend's aid. Sandy's safety net was complete.

Of course, the two friends couldn't know that by the end of their third year of college, Sandy wouldn't be able to see at all. An ophthalmologist's misdiagnosis led to glaucoma, and Sandy went from 20/20 vision at the start of freshman year to 0/0 at the end of junior year.

The options for a suddenly blind young man, especially in the early 1960s, were not plentiful. He could join his father in the junk business, become a justice of the peace in the hinterlands of western New York state, or make screwdrivers or cane chairs. "And that," Sandy says now, "was to be my fate."

When Art reminded his buddy of their promise to each other, Sandy insisted that this was different; it didn't count. Nor did he want Sue's future cut short just because his future had been. He told Sue and Art to move on and forget about him. "I had no money, no prospects, no eyes, no future," he recalls thinking. Neither Sue nor another childhood friend, Sandy Hoffman, would give up on him.

Art wouldn't give up on him either. "You don't understand," said Art, walking with Sandy back in Buffalo. "You are my best friend. I need you." Eventually, Art convinced Sandy to return to Columbia, promising he would be Sandy's eyes. He would even help him find his way through the streets of Manhattan.

Up to a point.

One day in New York City, Sandy and Art went downtown for Sandy's appointment with a case worker at an institute for the blind. When it was time to leave, Art—an architecture student—said he needed to sketch a building for an assignment, and asked Sandy to wait.

Sandy was dumbfounded. He panicked. He needed to get back to Columbia to meet a reader, and he had no choice but to head back on his own. He didn't think he could do it, but Art insisted he had to stay and do the drawing. Terrified, Sandy made his way to the subway and began his trek back uptown.

As he journeyed north, Sandy bumped into strangers, walked into poles and bloodied his face, and nearly fell onto the subway tracks. After the most harrowing hour of his life, he finally made it back through the gates of Columbia—and felt a tap on his shoulder.

It was Art.

He had been there the whole time, just far enough behind to make sure Sandy was okay, but keeping his distance to help Sandy realize he could do the thing that scared him most.

Sandy went on to finish Columbia (Phi Beta Kappa), pursue a Marshall Scholarship at Oxford University, receive his master's and his doctorate at Harvard, and acquire his MBA back at Columbia. He even did his delayed stint in the White House, and he later chaired the federal Rural Healthcare Corporation and served on the National Science Board. His path to becoming an entrepreneur and investor began with his invention of a compressed speech machine, which transformed tape recordings by speeding up the reproduction of words without distortion; it continued when he created the first global database for tracking antibiotic resistance.

His roommate, of course, went on to join Paul Simon in forming the blockbuster folk duo Simon & Garfunkel.

Today, Sandy chairs the board of the Wilmer Eye Institute at Johns Hopkins, and has instituted a prize for research aiming to end blindness worldwide. His life story is told in his autobiography, *Hello Darkness, My Old Friend*—the opening lyric from the classic Simon & Garfunkel tune "The Sound of Silence." Sandy's friend and neighbor Ruth Bader Ginsburg wrote the book's foreword, and novelist Margaret Atwood penned its afterword.

And he remains happily married to Sue to this day. Not too shabby for someone who, at nineteen years old, assumed he had no options.

Sandy thought he had a safety net, until everything comfortable fell away and nothing seemed safe anymore. That's when he began to fly.

ARE YOU READY FOR THIS RIDE?

Daring to fly high on the Trapeze doesn't always happen with the greatest of ease. The pulse quickens, the sweat trickles, the stomach flip-flops—and you're not sure whether it's from excitement or terror. When taking your act to the next level, dangling precariously from the high bar, which emotion you go with is up to you. Why not choose excitement?

Dream bigger! Try new things! In this big improvisation called "life," another option always comes swinging your way—and it's yours for the taking. Let go of the illusion that a safety net is what's keeping you safe. All along, it was the perfectly imperfect you.

As you leap from your perch and reach for that next swing, consider the following questions:

- How did things work out the last time you tried something new?
- What part of your track record can prepare you for this next uncertain opportunity?
- Have you learned more from perfection or from imperfection?

Finding Your Own Way

★

Climb aboard the Scrambler, but hold on to your hat! Soon you'll be whirling and twirling, spiraling and swirling, feeling dizzier and more dazed with each revolution. Nothing makes sense when you're rotating in every direction and—surprise!—there's no clear path ahead. Finally, just when things look their most confusing, the frenzy stops, and the way out appears: through making choices that matter to *you*.

Admitting What You Love

Brad Meltzer had expected the first twenty-two rejections of his debut novel's manuscript, but the twenty-third and twenty-fourth submissions were supposed to be different. "There's going to be a bidding war," his agent had promised, sending Brad home to wait for the phone call that would get him out of debt. But when the call came, all he heard was: "Sorry, kiddo."

Instead of giving up, Brad started again. *If they didn't like that book, I'll write another*, he thought. *And if they don't like that book, I'll write another.*

"I was young and stupid and stubborn," he says today. But that insistence on pushing through adversity helped him publish his first book, *The Tenth Justice*, as a *New York Times* best seller.

Growing up, Brad didn't even know what the *New York Times'* "Best-Seller List" was. There were no books in his childhood home; he jokes that his parents read seven books in their whole lives, seven Brad had published by the time they passed away. Even after that journey from novice to success, Brad thought the road from *Sorry, kiddo* to best seller would be the most difficult he would have to navigate—but that was nothing compared with the pressure of delivering his follow-up second novel, *Dead Even*.

Again, he thought it would end there. Successful debut, check! Successful follow-up, check! But even after he continued to publish novel after best-selling novel, Brad had doubts about each new project. *Sorry, kiddo . . . Sorry, kiddo . . . Sorry, kiddo* rang in his ears.

"It's not that I need mountains to conquer," he says. He just doesn't want to let down all those involved in making his dreams a reality: the publisher, marketers, publicists. Worrying about their faith in him haunts him more than whether he ever gets another number one. And he tries not to even imagine disappointing his readers.

One day over lunch with fellow novelist David Baldacci, Brad sheepishly owned up to his feelings, and his feelings about his feelings. Yes, he was stressed, but he also felt like a jerk about stressing over the pressures of his success.

"I was worried about complaining that it was hard," he confesses. "Only a terrible, terrible person would complain about something so amazing!" After all, someone was paying him to create fascinating stories about imaginary people, and those stories had brought him great financial security. "If I complain about how hard this is," he asked, "what kind of thankless asshole am I?"

Baldacci just looked at him and replied, "Brad, if it was easy, everyone would do it."

A light bulb switched on in Brad's head. His response to his doubts had been all wrong. Not only was it permissible to admit that finding his way again and again through the work was hard, but it was in fact a sign of something crucial. Brad was doing something that demanded he continue to bring his best every day. And the fact that he wanted to do just that was an indication that he had found the work he loves most of all.

"To keep chasing that thing you want in life, you've got to admit what you love, and that opens you up to a really scary place," he explains. "Because then if you don't get it, you're heartbroken." Yet that level of emotional commitment, he firmly believes, is the only way to ever really get what you want.

Nearly three decades in, Brad has gotten what he was chasing and more, including twelve best-selling thrillers; a collection of award-winning children's books; and multiple television and film projects spanning topics including historical figures, conspiracy theories, and real-life heroes. But he isn't done yet, and he never wants to lose that energy and passion he started with.

So every single day that he sits down to write, he replays in his head that crucial moment when he could've called it quits: *Sorry, kiddo. Sorry, kiddo. Sorry, kiddo.*

"And that drives me," he insists. "That's rocket fuel for me."

Keep Making Your Art

Not everyone has a famous author who gives measured and reasonable opinions—not even close. Most of us are surrounded by people all too willing to offer unwanted feedback and unsolicited advice. And when we tell them about our next big, hairy, audacious goal, expecting enthusiasm or at least a tiny nod of approval, instead we get a wet blanket.

Maybe it's coming from a place of love. Old friends or family members hear your outrageous (and possibly unrealistic) dreams and think, *Oh, the* you *I knew ten years ago would get hurt. I should stop you.* But the last time you lived in the same house as your parents, you probably put empty milk cartons back in the fridge, left the family car to run on fumes, and littered the living room with dirty socks. You didn't have a fully developed frontal lobe. So, it begs the question: Do these people from your past really know you or what you're capable of doing today? Doubtful.

Maybe it's coming from a place of jealousy. Perhaps you have someone in your life who will judge their rise only by your stagnation—or even your fall. Whether that person is in the next cubicle or on the next yoga mat, their scarcity mindset won't allow them to bathe in the glow of your achievement. From somewhere deep in the bowels of camaraderie and friendship, their jealousy wakes up and whispers, *Why you and not me?*

Or maybe it's coming from a place of fear, like when you run into a friend at the coffee shop and tell her of your crazy new dream, and she says,

"You can't do that! That's so scary!" But what she really means is, *I can't do that! I'm too scared!*

These aren't bad people; they just aren't *your* people. So, don't feel bound to listen to them. Focus instead on what you do best—whatever you're building, creating, innovating, and willing into existence.

As you're navigating your next Wonderhell, you must make an important choice: Who gets to tell you what you can and can't do? Stop giving votes to people in your life who shouldn't even have a voice. The only one who really has a say is the one who knows you best: you.

You get to decide what you share, and with whom. Just as important, you get to decide *when* you share it. Your response to each opportunity or hurdle is totally up to you.

Got a family member who always worries you're taking too big a risk? Share some details of your plan when you've already got it in place.

Got a friend who doesn't believe you have the courage to start some new project? Tell her only after you've gotten the ball rolling.

Got a colleague who pokes holes in your proposal because he wants to be the center of attention? Ask him what ideas he would contribute and conscript him to become invested in your success.

Meanwhile, keep plugging away, regardless of what others choose to think or do.

Bear in mind: most of the people who are busy sharing opinions wouldn't have the time to do so if they were just as busy as you, bringing their own goals to fruition. As pioneering pop artist Andy Warhol advised, stop worrying about all those people, and just keep going. After all, he moved to the beat of his own drummer and, in doing so, created a whole new school of art. Did he have doubts? Probably. And did he let those doubts stop him? Not one bit.

"Don't think about making art, just get it done," Warhol once said. "Let everyone else decide if it's good or bad, whether they love it or hate it. While they are deciding, make even more art."

Make It Tattoo-Worthy

Seth Godin, the world-renowned marketing expert, likes to talk about the difference between a brand and a lifestyle. A brand, he explains, is something that you buy because it's the convenient, cost-effective, and logical choice. But a lifestyle is something that you'll go out of your way to purchase, spending more time and money than you might otherwise, because of the emotional value conveyed to you through ownership.

Being a Harley-Davidson rider, for example, is a lifestyle. People ride Harley-Davidson motorcycles, wear Harley-Davidson gear, get Harley-Davidson tattoos. Suzuki, on the other hand, is a brand. Think about it for a minute: I bet you've never seen a Suzuki tattoo. "Harley-Davidson is committed, in every choice, to making itself tattoo-worthy," says Seth.

You can imagine how tickled I was, upon running into Seth at an event, to share with him a photo of a woman who tattooed the cover art from my book *Limitless* on her arm.

Tara Diab was one of the people I profiled in *Limitless*. When the book came out, she said I'd captured her life and her potential in a way that was so near and dear to her, she never wanted to forget it. So, she put it on her arm in permanent ink, in a place of honor—right next to the tattooed aviation wings of her late father, a military pilot.

When Tara sent me the video showing off her new tattoo and describing her reasons for getting it, I gasped. I couldn't even speak. Being limitless was her lifestyle, I realized—and suddenly, I felt responsible. My ideas were tattoo-worthy. They mattered to someone. That meant I had to get them right.

Your words matter. Your actions matter. Your work matters.

The world pays attention to Harley-Davidson. Tara pays attention to me. And someone—a friend, a colleague, a child, a total stranger in a momentary, random act of attention—is paying attention to you, too, even if you don't always know it. You are somebody to someone. You owe it to those people to make sure what you do is wise, true, and good.

As you find your way along the narrow road from your past accomplishments to your future endeavors—as you make your own art, in whatever form—never lose sight of that purpose. Make sure that kernel of an idea is meaningful enough to display somewhere permanently and prominently. Imagine it on a shoulder, a wrist, or an ankle!

By dropping the news of this responsibility, I'm placing a lot of the hell on you. But the way through that hell—the way to get it right—is to take it seriously. Know what you want to work toward *more than anything else*. Know why you do it, and who you do it for. That's the wonder.

To move forward on your own path through the doubt and the unknown, you must be forever willing to work hard at what you love, over and over. And sometimes that work weighs on you; it weighs on me, too. I feel the burden of my ego—of getting everything right, of wanting not to let anyone down. When this happens to Brad, he repeats, *Sorry, kiddo,* to remind him of his true north. I just look at Tara's bicep and remember why all the hard work is worth it.

Cultivate an Abundance Mindset

A landmark Stanford University study once tested young children's ability to exercise patience and logic over immediate satisfaction.[1] You might recognize this study by its widely known description: the marshmallow test.

Each child sat alone in a room at a desk with a small tin holding a marshmallow and a choice: they could eat one marshmallow now, or wait fifteen minutes and get *two* marshmallows. The team of psychologists then followed these children for years after administering the marshmallow test. The children who were able to delay gratification had better educational outcomes, brain development, and prefrontal cortex activity (which implies more varied, complex behaviors and organization) than those who did not.

We know now that other factors, such as family and economic background, influence the ability to delay gratification.[2] Yet one thing remains true: The children who spent their time staring only at the marshmallow were more likely

---

1 Walter Mischel and Ebbe B. Ebbesen, "Attention in Delay of Gratification," *Journal of Personality and Social Psychology*, 1970.
2 Tyler W. Watts, Greg J. Duncan, and Haonan Quan, "Revisiting the Marshmallow Test: A Conceptual Replication Investigating Links Between Early Delay of Gratification and Later Outcomes," *Psychological Science*, 2018.

to eat it during the first fifteen minutes. The ones who distracted themselves—by covering their eyes, resting their head on their arms, singing songs, inventing games, or even trying to fall asleep—fared better on the original test's metrics.

Maybe in the past, you would have settled for that one marshmallow. But things have changed. *You* have changed. Now, that second marshmallow is not only within your reach, but within your power.

We know that to find what fuels us, we need to focus inward.

We know that to figure out what matters, we need to focus outward.

But we also need to be able to distract ourselves by focusing elsewhere, so we can stay the course longer and ultimately perform better.

So, how do we stay the course when doubt, disruption, and deficiency continually persuade us to see only the most immediate type of fulfillment? By choosing an abundance mindset, and refusing to let our fear of losing one marshmallow prevent us from gaining two.

You can encourage a mindset of abundance in many ways. Write in a gratitude journal. Focus on possibility more than risk. But the most effective way is to serve others, creating opportunities where you aren't the only winner—making sure success and marshmallows are available for everyone.

When you are pulling yourself up from the bottom, it may be tempting to keep score and see the world in terms of *me versus you*. Every Success Bully out there will tell you that if you're not screwing someone else, you're getting screwed. This fear—that there isn't enough to go around—comes from a scarcity mindset, and it affects your decision-making.

But the Success Bullies are wrong. An outlook built around *never enough* increases attention toward the scarce resource while undermining the importance of long-term gain elsewhere.[3] Land grabs yield frustrated energy, and pursuing this path as you look forward will, at best, make you look selfish.

You can pursue both strategy *and* service; one doesn't necessarily come at the price of the other. And finding balance between the two can help you find your way through Wonderhell.

---

3 Inge Huijsmans et al., "A Scarcity Mindset Alters Neural Processing Underlying Consumer Decision Making," *Proceedings of the National Academy of Sciences of the United States of America*, 2019.

Opportunities to be of service—in your community, your business, your personal life—are always plentiful. What can you do today, this week, this month, for free or at a low cost, that provides value for others? How can you use the external data from such work? How might your service demonstrate your brilliance or be an effective way to sharpen your tools and shape your path forward?

There may be no line on your P&L for it, but these opportunities will pay dividends. Cultivating an abundance mindset will warm your heart, show your character, and create authentic bonds with employees, customers, and friends.

In each new Wonderhell, you will experience a daily (or maybe hourly) moment of panic. But if you focus on what you have (instead of what you don't) and consider how you can be of service to others, you'll be able to turn that one marshmallow into something much greater.

Driving Your Own Process

Tiffani Bova decided that being of service was also a way to get better at her craft. Sure, she has an enviable group of advisors around her, from entrepreneurial "evangelist" Guy Kawasaki (who pushed her to improve her presentations) to marketing guru Seth Godin (who pushed her to write a book) to Arianna Huffington (who helped Tiffani start the journey of giving back to an industry that had been so good to her). But her circle of trusted advisors doesn't stop with these famous names. To take charge of her own process, she decided to listen to hundreds of other people every week.

In 2019, Tiffani flew 275,000 miles to give one hundred keynote speeches on six different continents as the chief global growth evangelist for Salesforce and the author of the *Wall Street Journal* best seller *Growth IQ*. It was a busy year, although it looked a lot like her previous ten years, too. To say she is a popular speaker would be a serious understatement.

"When I started speaking," Tiffani insists, "I was not very good." It was 2006, and she was addressing five hundred people from behind a podium at a conference in Houston, relying on her printed notes and her slides crammed with words. She would read her notes very seriously, then read the slide, then read her notes, over and over until finally she was done. Watching the recorded event afterward, she thought, *Whoa, that was really painful.* But she knew she could be better.

Tiffani decided to strike up a bargain. She would offer a copy of her presentation to anyone who provided substantive feedback. Tiffani wanted to know what people really thought about the substance of the presentation. And coming up with that tradeoff helped her hone the stories she went on to share in the future.

Now she could say, *That story fell flat,* or *That slide doesn't resonate—* or on the flip side, *People really liked this topic, and I should expand on it.* It was like having a focus group or her own little advisory board.

It also gave her more fodder for the next presentation. Each bit of feedback came with thoughts and ideas about what these individuals and their companies did that was interesting, innovative, and new, and those stories often found their way into Tiffani's future talks. People would say, "That's exactly what we are going through. It was almost like you were sitting in our leadership meeting!" and "How do you stay so close to the pulse?" It was because she was getting hundreds of emails a week, full of real-time feedback and real-world stories.

I know, I know . . . I just advised you to stop giving votes to people in your life who shouldn't have a voice. I mean, the subtitle of my previous book starts with "How to Ignore Everybody"! So why am I commending Tiffani for inviting hundreds of opinions from other people every single week? Because this clever move was an intentional part of Tiffani's strategy: to create a large enough data set that she could pick and choose useful tidbits from these collective voices and ask for perspectives on broader strategy questions from those voices she respected most.

Not content to muddle through discomfort or just "get by" the same way everyone else did, Tiffani took charge of her own process and became a student of her craft. By seeing each at-bat as an opportunity to improve, she found her own way through Wonderhell years ago. Now, fielding thousands of curveballs each year with grace and determination, she is pushing the edge and finding her own way still.

ARE YOU READY
FOR THIS RIDE?

Doubts and uncertainty can leave you scrambled. You're spinning fast, and you don't know which way is up, but you're determined to not lose your lunch on the Scrambler. You've found something you love—a goal that is worth your struggle. Your ego is talking: it has seen your potential, and it is hungry for more.

Living up to the burden of that newfound potential will feel less disorienting if you focus on why you do what you love, keep an eye on your ultimate goal, and ignore the critics who don't matter to you.

As you maneuver through this confusing moment, consider the following questions:

- When you tell people about your dreams, what emotions ground their reactions—and how do these resonate with your own?
- How are you judging the impact of your work?
- How can you show up for and serve others as you orient yourself toward the new you?

Gaining Perspective on Other People

★

Pull back, get a bird's-eye view, and see the bigger picture from the Ferris Wheel. From below, this human roulette looks straightforward—but as you climb, your perspective changes. Soar above it all and marvel at the panoramic vista from the top, where the dazzling heights offer fresh insights. Which people lift you up and belong in your life? Which ones drag you down and need to get gone? Circle back to ground level to say hello, and then maybe goodbye as you rise high into the sky.

Going All In

Trina Gray sailed through high school and college as a top student, athlete, and journalist—basically, an all-around leader. As she got older, she excelled at the right job, married the right guy, grew the right family. She was happy. She was successful. And she was exactly who she was supposed to be, until one day she wasn't.

Trina had always set the bar high for herself. She worked hard, studied hard, showed up hard, and was driven to be a leader in all parts of her life. But it wasn't the competition aspect that compelled her, even in athletics. "I was more interested in being part of something, being recognized for my leadership, and collaborating than I was obsessed with winning," she says.

This philosophy carried over off the field as well, where she consistently went all in. She went all in at college, acing her classes and earning the best internship. She went all in at work, landing a dream job upon graduation. She went all in for her family, marrying a great man right out of college and following his career to a small town in Michigan, where going all in for her children meant late-night work and red-eye flights to be there for both the important and the seemingly everyday (but no less important) events in their lives.

As Trina grew her family, as well as two thriving businesses—the national award–winning Bay Athletic Club and a top-ranked Beachbody coaching team—she knew who she was, she knew where she was going, and she knew how fast she wanted to get there. But she also knew that it would take a village to keep going at that pace. Having spent years going all in with her community, hosting trips, retreats, and opportunities for adventure and growth, her village was full of friends who went all in for her, too.

One of those friends was Erin. Trina and Erin had become close over a couple of years, working out together, paddleboarding, going out for coffee, drinks, and laughs. As busy moms, they found peace in each other. Then life took an unexpected turn: Trina and Erin fell in love.

It was hard enough for them to understand, much less others. But most people trusted that they knew themselves and would not drop a bomb on their lives if the love was not real. Most people celebrated their happiness.

Sure, it took more time for some to manage the unexpected changes and confusion. Trina's husband was hurt but kind. They adjusted to divorce and co-parenting. They remain friends and supporters. Her children adjusted to two households and other family changes, and stayed on their own path to success. Eventually, they all found their groove, and life carried on.

Even so, Trina still carries emotional scars inflicted by family members who didn't approve of her choices.

"You're pathetic. Go away and fix yourself. You're ruining your career and your kids' future. You're a bad mom. You're selfish. Go repent," they would decry. And then they'd ask, "How can you do this to your kids?"

"I'm not doing this *to* my kids," Trina replied. "I'm doing this *for* my kids."

And she kept going all in.

"I have no choice but to be who I am, and to live my life fully as this person," Trina says today. "I've always shown up hard, and now I also show up true." She learned to stop apologizing for growing. And she took a step back to gain perspective on who should—and who shouldn't—be in her family's life.

She learned to stop asking for permission to be who she was, and as a result, Bay Athletic Club thrived. Trina's Beachbody business thrived, too. Most important, her relationship with Erin and their children thrived—so much so that they got married in their backyard, surrounded by their children, their closest friends, family, and coworkers who spanned decades of their lives.

In rising to new heights, Trina lost some of those other people, including a few of her closest family members. (She still invited them to the wedding. They declined . . . but sent a fern.) But an overwhelming number of people stood by her side, all in. Why? Because she'd spent a lifetime going all in for them.

In Praise of Burning Bridges

This feels like the right moment to share an unpopular opinion: I'm in favor of burning bridges.

Anyone who knows me will attest that I am no diplomat. I do not seek shared ground. I do not exploit commonalities. "Blunt" is my middle name. All in, indeed.

Mind you, I am a yenta, a maven, and a matchmaker extraordinaire. I introduce, I open doors, I fix up. I have lifelong friendships built on decades of ill-advised adventures and walking together through fires. But I am zero parts charm offensive or bridge builder. On the contrary, I believe that sometimes a bridge needs to be burned.

I don't say this flippantly, and I don't take the decision to burn a bridge lightly. But when it needs to be done, it needs to be done.

As we encounter each new Wonderhell, in that moment between yesterday's accomplishment and tomorrow's dream, we often stop in our tracks, listening to lies in our heads and letting them deter our progress.

First, we tell ourselves not to take a risk, because this thing we want to do next isn't quite perfect, and we aren't quite ready.

Then, we tell ourselves not to make a leap because we might fail.

And then we tell ourselves that if we live the way we know we're meant to live, people won't like us.

The first and second warnings are born of fear and doubt. You can refute them easily enough: Sure, your plan isn't perfect, and you might not be ready. But it will never be perfect, and you'll never be ready. So why not start now? And sure, you might fail—most certainly you will, in fact. But don't fret! Make a loose plan instead for what you will do when (not if) that happens. And then get going!

But the third lie you tell yourself—*People won't like the real me*—is the one that really worries you, and that's because it's true. The lie isn't that they won't like you. The lie is that these people matter.

Some people will disapprove of the life you'd really like to be living. They won't like the *you* that you want to become. But why let them define your success? Why should they get a vote about what or who you should be?

Here is the truth bomb: when you grow—when your life gets bigger—you are inevitably going to outgrow the people who liked you when you were smaller.

Why? Perhaps, as discussed earlier, their designs on your progress come from a place of love, or jealousy, or fear. Or perhaps they feel insecure about their own choices. They perversely believe that your growth somehow limits their own. Whatever the reason, you may find that as you move forward, it's best to leave them behind.

Your potential is limitless. So why live in a way designed for the comfort of people who want to impose limits on you? And why respond this way to those particular people? Why should they decide whether or not your life is the right life . . . for you?

Go ahead, burn that bridge. Or at least stop checking it every day.

It's Okay to Unfollow People (and in Real Life, Too)

This just in from the Department of the Obvious: social media is bad for you. So, after you've burned that bridge, unfollow the toxic person in question on social media, too.

Social media makes our noisy world even noisier. It comes between you and your goals, your success, your happiness. It sucks up your time, doling out tiny dopamine hits in scientifically proven, maximally addicting ways to keep you coming back for just one more, and one more, and one more . . . It stokes your worst traits, conjuring up jealousy, stirring up judgment, and swirling your petty tendencies into a poisonous froth.

Sure, it's a lifeline when we are physically distanced but yearn for connection. It can allows us to network with colleagues and develop professionally. But how much of what you get from social media is additive to your life, and how much is just a pointless diversion?

Prominent entrepreneur and motivational speaker Jim Rohn once reasoned that each of us is the average of the five people we keep closest to us. Although there are no studies that back up this arbitrary number, science shows that the people "closest" to you don't have to be physically close at all, and the number is irrelevant. To shape our thinking, change our trajectory, or impact our outcomes, these people simply have to siphon our attention. In other words, the people with whom we interact most, even on social media, count for a lot.

Did you know that people with overweight friends are 57 percent more likely to become overweight themselves, even if those friends live on the other side of the country? Your emotional connection, not your physical proximity, is the key factor. The behavior of your closest intimates—wherever they are— influences the way you behave.[1]

What *they* do becomes what *you* do.

What *they* think becomes what *you* think.

What *they* normalize becomes what *you* normalize.

---

1 Nicholas A. Christakis, MD, PhD, MPD, and James H. Fowler, PhD, "The Spread of Obesity in a Large Social Network Over 32 Years," *New England Journal of Medicine,* 2007.

So, go ahead; unfriend anyone who makes you doubt your dreams or prevents you from following a new path. Burn that social media bridge.

But if that's too difficult, awkward, or unfeasible, Dr. David Burkus—who studied networks for his book *Friend of a Friend: Understanding the Hidden Networks That Can Transform Your Life and Your Career*—offers a slightly different option. Extend the length of the bridge in real life, putting more distance between you and the person you'd like to leave behind.

Dr. Burkus and his wife hate feeling guilty about not spending time with people, so they made a short list and a long list. "Everyone we want to spend time with is on the short list, and everyone else is on the long list," he explains. For people who don't lift them up or bring something positive to the table, the Burkuses maintain a strict policy: *The phone works both ways.* "Then you can get really bad at even replying to them when they do reach out," he continues. "And eventually those people bring their negativity, their toxicity, and all that other stuff to a more willing recipient."

When it comes to these social bridges, extending their length can be just as useful as burning them. As it turns out, the people who affect you most are not just those five or so close friends, but also all the friends connected to those close friends. So, keep those unnecessary connections at a distance. Take a step back from your social set—both on and off the screen—to evaluate the people surrounding you, *and* the people surrounding them.

Who is influencing you in real life and on social media? Does seeing them or their posts bring you joy, knowledge, and connection? Do you aspire to be like them in some positive way? Or are they draining your energy, or forcing you into endless arguments that range from the irrelevant to the insane?

The crucial question is, do those people push you forward or hold you back? If it's the latter, I have one word for you: *unfollow, unfollow, unfollow.* Technically, that's three words, but this reflects just how important it is to disengage the energy vampires sucking away your vitality.

Consider who belongs in your community—the people whose actions, thoughts, and norms make you proud—and unfollow the rest. Once you've taken that step back and gained a little perspective from this new vantage point, you'll learn that goodbye can be a gift.

Goodbye Is a Gift

Why do we tremble at the idea of endings? Why do we hesitate when we know that we should sever ties?

Because we are scared and filled with doubt.

Because we are creatures of habit.

Because we think our self-worth is determined by others.

Because we feel unworthy of more.

Because we don't know how to fill the void.

Because we don't know what alternative awaits.

Because success is uncertain.

Because we think we're not ready to say goodbye.

I could go on, but the fact remains: we often cling to what we should banish.

As your vision for your next Wonderhell begins to emerge, a time will come when you must choose. You can't keep someone in your inner circle whose lack of imagination is limiting your ambition, whose stagnation is stopping your evolution, or whose fear is curbing your excitement—not if you want to get through the hell to the wonder, and become the person you know you can be. And this is where the gift of goodbye reveals itself.

Goodbyes allow you to put in the rearview mirror a habit that doesn't build you, a practice that doesn't grow you, a mindset that doesn't serve you, a belief that doesn't suit you, a friend who doesn't see you—I mean really, really *see* you. Goodbyes allow you to move forward into the uncertainty of your new perspective.

After trying for decades to change for those people who would never love me, I finally hit what my mother so aptly called the Fuck-You Forties. That's when I realized that some people love me, and some decidedly do not—and this is okay. I went to school on the points where I was in the wrong, and made my peace with those people. As for the others, I realized that I shouldn't be bothered, and I said goodbye wherever and whenever it was necessary.

Who appointed those unsupportive people judge and jury anyway? Just say goodbye already! The wheel of your progress will turn faster without all that deadweight.

We can do this with our habits, too.

Our society is so overwhelmed with get-rich-quick, get-thin-fast reinvention schemes that we've fallen for the biggest fallacies of all: that everyone else has the answer, and that we are only one decision away from a whole new life. Instead of leaping to the next thing to keep us busy or bring us a miracle, why not just let go of the current thing that isn't working? Why fool ourselves by hoping for results that we secretly know won't ever come so easily?

Stop saying *yes* simply because you're afraid to be alone with your *no.* Saying goodbye without knowing what's next can be your whole new lease on life.

You could say goodbye to that frenemy who makes you feel terrible, even without replacing her with ten new friends guaranteed to make you feel great.

You could say goodbye to too much screen time, even without picking out your next twelve perfect books to read instead.

You could say goodbye to sitting at your desk all day, even without a fourteen-point plan of how to achieve the greatest possible fitness.

Too often we don't make a change because we haven't figured out what's next. But you can let go of past things without needing to replace them with something new right away, even if it feels a bit uncomfortable at first. Likewise, you can make the conscious choice to be alone rather than in the wrong company.

Simplify, simplify! Goodbye is enough. No need for a new hello just yet. Sit in the uncertainty and discomfort and open space for a while. Say goodbye to the villains trying to dominate your story, and instead focus on the hero: you.

Firing Your Villain

Heather Monahan had to say goodbye. After fourteen years with the same media company, Heather had succeeded in every metric, earning three promotions all the way up to chief revenue officer. The CEO adored Heather. The president adored Heather. But the chief financial officer decidedly did not.

By her early forties, Heather had begun to feel an internal agitation about her larger purpose. She wanted more than just to make rich shareholders even richer. "I wanted to bring more good to light for people who grew up poor, like I had," she says now. She also wanted to model empowerment for women and show them that if she could get to the C-suite, so could they.

Heather built a side business as a consultant and speaker while continuing to crush every goal at her day job. The CFO, already not a fan, got wind of her side hustle and demanded that Heather take down her new website immediately. The CFO even brought in the general counsel, who told Heather that building a personal brand outside of work was a conflict of interest for the company.

But Heather is no dummy. She had already done her homework on the chief revenue officer at another well-known company, and he had a huge personal brand. "I had spoken to attorneys," she recalls. "I knew that you can have your own life online, outside of work." She agreed to change the language on her website to be extra-double-triple clear, but no way was Heather backing down.

This further inflamed the CFO's ire, until the CFO became outwardly aggressive and nasty. She would bad-mouth Heather behind her back, creating outlandish mandates and unrealistic expectations—like the time she ordered Heather, ten days after giving birth, to board a plane to give a major presentation. And Heather always said yes, not wanting to antagonize the CFO any further.

This went on for months, with the CFO growing in power and audacity while Heather shrank back further and capitulated more. When the CFO decided to fire her, Heather realized that she shared some of the blame. "We teach others how to treat us," she explains. And she decided to stand up for herself.

Heather was not going to be bullied any longer.

"The CFO called me into her office and pushed two pieces of paper across the desk," Heather recalls. "On one, it said, 'Heather Monahan has been fired.' On the other, it said a bunch of fluffy stuff about how I was beloved but decided to move on to a new adventure." That second statement came with a big check—and an even bigger nondisclosure, nondisparagement agreement. Heather hadn't written either one, so she wasn't signing either one. Instead, she walked out.

Heather renegotiated her typical response and showed up as a more powerful version of herself. Even as she spent the entire time fighting back tears, she knew it was the most badass thing she'd ever done. She was getting fired from her job, but she was also going to fire the villain from her life.

Saying goodbye to those who made her small meant Heather was able to say hello to making herself big. Because of her twelve-month noncompete contract, she couldn't approach anyone else in her industry, so no matter what industry she chose, she would have to start over as a rookie. "If I'm gonna roll the dice on someone," she recalls thinking, "I'm gonna roll the dice on me." She was afraid of what this new outlook would bring, but she moved ahead anyway toward whatever might come next.

Over the next five years, as Heather writes in her best-selling books *Confidence Creator* and *Overcome Your Villains*, her fear gave way to curiosity. Curiosity gave way to first steps. First steps gave way to competence. And competence gave way to confidence. A pattern of progress unfurled, and it all started by gaining perspective on who belonged in her life, and who needed to be left behind.

ARE YOU READY
FOR THIS RIDE?

You've reached the highest highs, and the view from the top of the Ferris Wheel has shown you what—and whom—to prioritize. Some people lift you up, but others are holding you down. Now you have some choices to make about who should stay with you and who must give up their seat.

If the people in your life aren't additive, it's time for a little subtraction. Although this can feel like a great unburdening, some goodbyes (especially from people who should have shown up for the real you all along) will be tinged with a wee bit of vertigo. But taking a stand and being brave enough to live as your truest self will push you to live through the hell and into the wonder, where you will find a long line of people who deserve to ride along with you.

As you ponder who gets to remain and who needs to go, consider the following questions:

- Does everyone in your life love, support, and celebrate the *you* that you truly want to be?
- Who has been in your life for far too long and needs to be pushed out (or at least pushed away)?
- What person, habit, or mindset do you need to leave behind, even if you are uncertain about what or who should replace it?

THE TUNNEL OF LOVE

Going Farther Together

★

Ride down into the Tunnel of Love, but be sure to snuggle up to the right partner. Whether it's a champion, a friend, a role model, or your favorite ass-kicker, your companion should be someone who shares your values and ambitions—someone who will talk you up, back you up, and never let you down. Because when the lights blink out and the boat starts rocking, you'll need to paddle together so you can go as fast and far as you know you can go.

Working Together Makes Things Work

Alan Mulally showed up for his first day as the new CEO of Ford Motor Company looking dapper in his khaki pants and blue blazer. The only problem: the automobile industry was decidedly blue pinstripe suits, pressed shirts, and pocket squares. That should have been the first indication to the corporate brass that things were about to change.

But that wasn't the only thing different about Alan. He was also the first person hired to run an American automobile company who didn't "grow up" in the industry. This might not have been such a big deal if, say, the auto industry was humming along. But it was not humming along. It was, at best, on life support.

Alan had been happily ensconced at Boeing, having begun as an engineer right out of college in 1969 and risen to the rank of CEO in the commercial airlines division, where he helped salvage the company after the catastrophic losses of 9/11. Alan holds multiple degrees in aeronautical and astronautical engineering, not to mention an MBA, but all he cared about was making the best airplanes in the world.

"That's how I wanted to serve," he says today. "I wanted to be the best engineer, checking in with everybody, doing my assignments, and getting feedback about what I could do better."

Early in his career, when Alan was assigned an engineer to manage, he started giving that engineer feedback, too. Lots and lots of feedback, until after fourteen rounds on one assignment, his engineer said, "Before you give me suggestions for improvement a fifteenth time, I would like to tell you that I'm quitting."

The engineer explained his frustration with Alan's tendency to micromanage. "Everyone here does 'command and control,' but that's not who you are," the engineer advised. "You are a really neat person who cares. You're going to be even more effective if you just be you."

Alan listened to this feedback and thought back to the lessons his parents had taught him.

The purpose of life is to love and be loved, in that order.
To serve is to live.
Seek to understand before you seek to be understood.
Expect the unexpected, and expect to deal with it.
Working together is the way to create a lot of good.
It's nice to be important, but it's more important to be nice.
Commit to lifelong learning and continuous improvement.
Develop one integrated life to deliver your life's work.

With all this in mind, Alan began to develop a leadership style that matched these values and called it Working Together. By the time he got to Ford nearly two decades later, his Working Together framework had become so crystallized that it fit neatly onto a single piece of paper.

Despite its roots in the mind of an astronautical engineer, Working Together isn't rocket science. It isn't command and control. It isn't micromanaging. It's just what it says it is—working together, and doing it by following just a handful of guidelines:

- Include everyone, all stakeholders ... and love 'em up.

- Do so with love, respect, positivity, and appreciation.

- Have a compelling vision, a comprehensive strategy, and relentless implementation against clear performance goals.

- Use facts and data to understand progress against one unified plan.

- Employ emotional resilience to trust the plan.

- Have fun! Enjoy the journey and each other.

At Ford, one of the first things Alan did was get rid of siloed management meetings, where mistakes were hidden, progress was inflated, and bad behavior was stoked. Instead, he brought every senior leader into the Thunderbird Room, posted a chart that displayed each one of their tasks, and asked them to apply a color code. Green meant things were going well. Yellow meant things were off track. Red meant things were in the danger zone.

At the first three meetings, where everyone was packed around the conference table, everything on the board was green. This stymied Alan's progress. "We are losing $17 billion per year," he said. "Everything can't be working perfectly."

Finally, one senior leader raised his hand and admitted that he had a problem.

"I was so excited!" Alan recalls, knowing what he had to do next: praise the employee, appreciate his honesty, open the floor to suggestions, and get his problem solved. But Alan also asked that particular leader to sit beside him at the next meeting as a sign to everyone else that candor and visibility would be valued in Alan's boardroom.

At that next meeting, the chart was awash in a sea of yellows and reds. With his unique leadership approach to getting the job done through collective accountability, Alan had started to build a team of people who would believe in and trust each other. Eventually, he proved that the way to turn Ford around was fundamentally the same as the key to saving Boeing: by working together.

Get Outside the Frame

The executives at Ford Motor Company are some of the best in the world; they just needed to feel confident that Alan Mulally saw this, too. The Working Together methodology allowed Alan to reflect back to them what he saw: that no matter the particular struggles in each division, together they comprised a group of talented, hardworking individuals. That was all it took to win them over.

My friends laugh that I, too, have an uncanny ability to win people over—to talk people into doing all manner of things, from running their own business to running a marathon to running for office. I don't talk people into doing these things because I like toying with them. No, I use my superpower for good, not evil. I become so confident *for* them that my confidence becomes contagious *to* them.

But it *is* a superpower. Like Alan did with his executives, I can see a person's potential and reflect it back in ways that he or she can finally believe, and maybe even start to act upon. I don't talk people into going after what *I* want. I talk them into going after what *they* want.

To be honest, all it takes is recognizing the sparkle in your eyes when discussing something you really want, something you're really in love with. Your whole face brightens. Your body language perks up. Your voice lowers to a reverent whisper or rises to an excited vibration. That shift is the tell—and suddenly I know you would work hard for it, even if you think achieving it is only a remote possibility.

Seeing that spark in someone else is easy. Seeing it in yourself is not.

Sometimes, when you can't see your own Wonderhell, you need to step back and look at things through someone else's eyes. It's hard to see the whole picture when you're inside the frame. And you, my friend, are inside of the frame, just as I am inside mine. All of us are trapped by what we think is possible, and yet what seems possible is based only on where we've been and what has been possible so far.

The human memory is short. We are basically fruit flies with stories. We forget how far we've come. We see only where we are now, and what overwhelming obstacle stands in front of us. Crushed by the hell of the slog ahead, we forget to reward ourselves for getting this far—or to use those advances to power our confidence for living into the wonder.

This is why it's so startling, so humbling, so terrifying—and so helpful—when someone we respect looks us square in the eyes and says, "You can do more."

You already know this. It's just that you have been unable to believe it or fully admit it to yourself. But that other person is seeing you from outside the frame, in your full, unvarnished, unclouded potential. You see the stuck-in-the-present you; that other person sees the potential future you.

This isn't just some motivational palaver, either. Science backs it up.

One 2004 study has shown that people who say, "I smoke," are more likely to quit smoking than people who say, "I am a smoker."[1] See the difference? The former is interpreted as a fleeting, momentary action, while the latter is seen as a fixed, unchangeable fate.

So, when someone outside of your frame sees you smoke—or order two desserts, or get a little too drunk, or show up late for a meeting—they don't see all the years you've been smoking or overeating or drinking or procrastinating. They just see the one moment in time, the single mistake. Their perspective isn't weighed down by the baggage of your history, your failed attempts, or your brain chemistry. They see nothing holding you back.

On the journey through Wonderhell, everyone could use a little company. If you choose your inner circle with care, they'll be the ones who see you in all your possibility. And nothing is better than that.

Not Better Than That

In 2019, I climbed Mount Everest. Except not really.

I climbed New England's Mount Stratton seventeen times in a row, for a total of 29,029 feet of accumulated elevation: the height of Mount Everest. But I didn't tell anyone about it in advance, and I didn't really train

---

1 Ildiko Tombor et al., "Smoker Identity and Its Potential Role in Young Adults' Smoking Behavior: A Meta-Ethnography," *Health Psychology,* 2015.

or prepare for it. Frankly, before I started, the whole thing seemed kind of silly, even a little embarrassing.

In *Limitless*, I profiled Alison Levine, who climbed Everest not once, but twice. In comparison, I saw my trek as a privileged, weekend-warrior, fashion-fitness boondoggle of simulated conditions to make you feel like a tough guy amid a whole lot of glamping creature comforts.

Yeah, I was wrong about all that. (And yeah, I definitely should have trained.)

Here's what it actually was: ice and snow and mud and slime and wind and guts and grit and tenacity and blisters and joy and community and exhaustion and determination and fellowship and love. It was highs, it was lows, and it was rapid-fire whiplash between the two with every single slogging-uphill step. It was physically challenging, but that paled in comparison to the mental and emotional evisceration.

About two-thirds of the way up the first ascent, I had a technical problem with one of my poles and asked a random stranger for help. His name was Monty, and he was climbing with friends from Texas who were going to spread the ashes of one of their brethren at the top of the mountain. We got to talking, and then two guys walking behind us joined the conversation. Shawn, who served in the US Army in Iraq, was from Pennsylvania and hiking to raise money for veterans. Matt from New York was doing the seventeen hikes as a fundraiser for a foundation in honor of Harris, a dear family friend who died from cancer at age seventeen.

At the aid station atop the mountain, we grabbed a few *stroopwafels*. We tried to fuel up on them while riding the gondola down, but with the 25-degree summit conditions, they were frozen solid. So we put them in our pockets for the next ascent, figuring they'd warm up. And #TeamPocketWaffles was born.

We spent the next sixteen hours pushing and pulling each other up the mountain that first day. Leave no Pocket Waffle behind! The Navy SEALs have a saying when they go about clearing a room: *Slow is smooth, and smooth is fast.* That became our motto for the entire climb.

Climb four times, then four more, then change into dry socks.

Strap on a headlamp and complete two more in the dark, before taking a thirty-minute break for dinner.

Commit to two more climbs, after most people had packed it in for the day, in the pitch-dark and wind and ice.

Take a nap, and then start again as the sun comes up the next morning.

The hardest thing about doing this hard thing wasn't the *hard*. It was the *doing*.

Sets of four, keeping your mind on where your feet are.

Just one climb, four times, four times over for sixteen.

Slow, smooth, fast.

That last one—climb number seventeen—was emotionally free. It was just a victory lap.

Of the 235 participants, 69 percent finished. Some were former professional football players and Navy SEALs. Others were world-record holders for casual things like running across the Sahara or trekking solo on foot across Antarctica. Still others were just, you know, athletes who run those little ultra-endurance races like Last Man Standing or the Leadville Trail 100 Run. And some were regular people like me.

"I am so glad you fellas are doing this with me," I said on one of those late-night trips up the mountain, speaking into the never-ending frigid darkness, "because I couldn't have done it alone."

At that point, a self-appointed human-potential guru who had been tagging along for our night climbs stopped me (and my forward progress, damn it!) to provide some unsolicited life coaching: "Come on, now! Do you want to be the person who thinks they couldn't do this alone? You're better than that!"

But I had to respectfully disagree. "Better than thinking I'm stronger because I have a pack that supports each other?" I asked. "Nope, I'm quite exactly as good as that, and proud of it."

Leaning on Team Pocket Waffles taught me that each of us is better when we gather a team to support us as we reach for the top. That team got me through my very own Everest.

You have an Everest, too, and you'll get to the top in your own way. One foot in front of the other. Sets of four. Slow is smooth, and smooth is fast.

Through the tunnel of darkness and into the light up ahead. Just keep moving forward, confident in the knowledge that your team is willing to do anything to support you on your climb—or to die trying.

Who's Your Ride or Die?

If you want to get something done, make a public commitment to complete it by a certain date. That's the advice of every nonsense-filled, supposedly motivational productivity article on the interweb. And sure, with that method, you'll slog through and get that big project done. But is simply getting it done good enough?

What if you could get it done in a way that makes you proud? For that, it's not enough to publicly commit to a *date*; you need to commit to a *person*, too. And that person should be the biggest ass-kicker you know: your Ride or Die.

Like the big goal you've just set, your Ride or Die should terrify you a bit, in all the best ways. Knowing this ass-kicker is there, waiting to see what you can do, should make you want to deliver something worthy of that person's time and attention. And if the thought of that person giving you honest, perhaps even painful feedback isn't pushing you to be better than you think possible—you need a new Ride or Die.

Here is the beauty of choosing a Ride or Die: in the process of striving to do work worthy of that person (or group of people), you set a new high bar for work that is worthy of yourself, too. The right Ride or Die won't just stop you from settling for mediocrity; this person will push you to discover your next Wonderhell.

My coaching clients tell me all the time that just knowing I'd be reading their journals, tracking their progress, and seeing their work made them take that extra time, complete that extra step, add that extra flourish. Although they hated me for it sometimes, in the end they learned that they were capable of so much more.

How often have you heard that success is an inside job—that you just have to want it badly enough, commit to it, and get up every day to do the damned thing? Well, if you're like me, sometimes you'd rather just stay in bed and skip the damned thing! What makes me go farther isn't some vague commitment to myself. I move better when I'm working together with my inner circle.

Who is in *your* inner circle?

Does your inner circle include an ass-kicker—a Ride or Die—for your newly expanded potential? If each new Wonderhell demands a leveling up, so should that inner circle. It should include someone you admire, someone to whose level of accomplishment you aspire.

Does your inner circle also include someone you can mentor? There is no better way to finally get past impostor syndrome at each new success than to spend some time teaching something you really, really know to someone new.

Finally, does your inner circle include a peer? This should be someone on a similarly new level or with similar new goals, someone with whom you can celebrate triumphs and commiserate over disappointments. A partner in crime keeps you moving forward without feeling alone, and provides a sanity check when things get overwhelming.

It may seem overwhelming to put together this team and then to constantly reevaluate and repopulate it with the right partners, but it doesn't have to be. Think of it this way. If exploring this new territory means you'll need to ask someone to join your inner circle as your Ride or Die, shouldn't *their* inner circle include someone to mentor?

Psst! That's you.

Staking Out New Territory

Tameka Fryer Brown had an epiphany, and she needed an inner circle to make it real.

One evening, while reading a picture book to her daughter, Tameka thought: *I could do this.* After doing some research, she learned something surprising: most children's stories that feature Black characters were written by white authors who didn't look like her.

"They are white people writing through a white lens," Tameka explains. "For publishing to prioritize that lens is problematic because it doesn't allow Black people to control our own narrative, to tell our stories in our way for our children." For Tameka, who wanted to create a legacy—for herself, for her family, and for her community—that would not stand.

Tameka was a good writer and had always loved children's books, but suddenly she felt it was even more important to tell stories that felt authentic. She was excited, but she had little idea of the difficulties ahead. She'd have to learn how to write picture books, sell them, and get her foot in the door of the publishing industry. For an inexperienced Black author with no track record, all those things would be a challenge—particularly in a publishing industry that was 80 percent white.

She couldn't do it by herself.

Tameka found an agent who could walk her manuscript into a publishing house—an impossible feat for an unpublished author working alone. Together, they sold two of Tameka's books for publication. And that was just the beginning.

Tameka knew that she had more in her, but she sensed that this agent was pushing her to sound like every other author, not empowering her to find that expanded potential. "She was a lot more editorial," Tameka says. "I had to go through so much to get my manuscript from her desk to a publisher." That worked when Tameka was new and didn't quite know herself as a writer, but after eight years of working together, she had found her own voice and wanted to see what else she could do. For that, she needed a new agent.

Still, Tameka was afraid to part ways with the person who had helped her navigate the unknown. When that agent decided to reduce her practice load, however, she did what Tameka had been too full of doubt to do: cut ties.

This gifted Tameka the time to consider what she wanted now that she was a more seasoned author. She sent queries to only three potential agents. The very next day, one of them contacted her and said, "I'm a big fan of your work. Let's talk."

Letting go of a fading relationship can feel a bit like walking over the edge of a cliff. It's terrifying to step out into the unknown. But taking that leap was the only way for Tameka to really stand on new ground.

Her new agent is a sounding board, a partner, a therapist—everything she never knew she needed. Together, they strategized to stake out new territory and guide Tameka's career, so she could write authentic stories that allow her unique voice to be heard.

Published in 2020, Tameka's book *Brown Baby Lullaby* was chosen as one of the New York Public Library's top children's books, one of NPR's 100 Best Books for Young Readers, and one of Amazon's Books of the Year. Tameka knows she couldn't have accomplished all this alone. She did it by leveling up her inner circle so she could go farther and faster to find a voice that both she and her readers truly loved.

ARE YOU READY FOR THIS RIDE?

As you enter the Tunnel of Love, choose your companions wisely. Rather than risk the tunnel vision of seeing only your present and past selves, travel this unfamiliar passageway with trusted partners who truly see *you* and glimpse the light ahead—your promise, your potential, your future.

Having someone in your boardroom, at your side, in your corner illuminates the way and shows you a different version of yourself—one that includes not just all you have been but all you can be. Recognizing who belongs in your inner circle, and trusting them on your next great adventure, gives you the momentum that makes doing the hard thing a bit less hard.

As you prepare to float through the shadows toward your next endeavor, moving farther than you ever thought possible, consider the following questions:

- Who in your life sees your potential, not just your past?
- Who is helping pull you up the mountain, and who are you helping to push?
- Who is in your inner circle, and who needs to be (or doesn't)?

THE LOOP-DE-LOOP

Adopting a
Beginner's Mindset

Standing Tall When the
Floor Drops Out

BUMPER CARS

Quieting Perfectionist
Tendencies

whack
a MOLE

Focusing on
What Matters

the
carousel

Saying No to Hustleporn

BURNOUT CITY

YOU
ARE
HERE

BURNOUT CITY

DO IT ALL OVER
AGAIN

You've made it through Impostortown, where you gave yourself permission and owned up to your next big dream, and Doubtsville, where you confronted mixed emotions and forged ahead. Now you know that you truly do belong on this new, bigger stage. And you've even gotten comfortable with being uncomfortable as you pursue those bigger dreams.

But wait! Wonderhell has one more magical island of fun to discover. Ahead lies Burnout City—where you get to do it all over again.

You thought success was a finite destination? That would mean there is a finite limit to your growth. Good news: you're not done learning. Bad news: you're not done learning.

Success is a cyclical journey, but holding on to your purpose while facing each fresh challenge is exhausting. Past successes and future prospects alike weigh heavy on your mind: *Should I cave to the pressure of bigger, better, faster, more? How can I make everything perfect when I am being pulled in every direction? And what do I do when disaster strikes?*

Wonderhell isn't just a place you visit once. If you have a vision (and the stomach for going after it), you get to come back over and over again. Anticipate this repeat voyage—and even welcome it!—and you'll live to tell the tale.

But the key isn't just to survive Wonderhell.

Your goal is to thrive in it.

Saying No to Hustleporn

★

Tickets, please, for the Carousel! This whimsical merry-go-round offers a moment of peace and serenity—a well-deserved respite after all the *go-go-go!* The question is: Do you stay here and float with the painted ponies, or do you hustle right back into the fray? And how do you even make that decision anyway? Sit back, relax, and regroup as the calliope plays, and remember why you started on this bold new path in the first place—and what is truly important to you.

It's about T-I-M-E

Jordan Harbinger is so good at uncovering the stories, skills, and secrets of the world's most interesting people that more than fifteen million people download his podcast conversations each month. He has interviewed the likes of basketball great Kobe Bryant, astrophysicist and teacher Neil deGrasse Tyson, and Google bigwig Eric Schmidt. But Jordan wasn't always in podcasting. He started off as a successful corporate lawyer on Wall Street, a job title synonymous with *hustle* if ever there was one.

One day Jordan noticed that Dave, the law partner who had hired him, wasn't hustling in the way all partners and partner-wannabes thought necessary to keep up with the crush of the billable-hour life. In fact, Dave was hardly ever in the office, spending his time instead attending charity events and playing squash. After a while, Jordan realized that Dave was more interested in lifestyle than law, using his work hours to build and manage personal relationships that allowed him to close deals worth millions of dollars for the firm—and lots of bonuses and flexibility for himself.

In Jordan's life experience, the path to success had been paved with hard work, but Dave didn't operate that way. Dave was using a strategy of working to live, not living to work. If this was a secret door to success, no one in law school had shared it with Jordan. He needed to know more.

So began Jordan's obsession with social psychology, networking, influence, persuasion, body language, and nonverbal communication. In uploading what he learned to the internet, Jordan accidentally became one of the first podcasters, eventually leaving the law firm to pursue his new passion full time and growing his podcast into one of the most successful in the world.

Jordan was at the top of his game, with big-time stars, big-time sponsorships, and a big-time listenership. He started wondering whether he should be doing even more, following the *bigger, better, faster, more* pressure all around him. Luckily for him, he had people to ask.

Jordan usually interviewed authors, speakers, course creators, and event hosts for his podcast at a time when they were promoting their next big thing—when they were in their newest Wonderhell. What Jordan heard from these big-time stars was always the same.

This is the hard part, the nightmare part.

This is the part where I don't see my spouse or kids for weeks on end.

I probably could have made the same amount of money if I'd just stayed home and advanced a new project instead of living on the road and hustling like this.

Yet even after sharing their torment and distress, the big-time stars shot the same questions back at Jordan, over and over and over.

Man, why are you leaving all that money on the table?

Where are all your paid courses?

Where are your live events and your speaking tour?

How come you don't have a book?

Jordan, full of doubt, began to ask himself those questions, too. But he loved his wife. He loved his growing family. And he loved the very good living he was making, doing exactly what he wanted to do—employing six full-time people, and producing excellent conversations on fascinating topics with interesting people. And so he said, "Nah, I'm good."

Rather than spending all of his time working so he could maximize his earnings, Jordan decided to spend just enough time working so he could maximize his time with his family. "Kids spell love T-I-M-E," he reasoned. "The less time you have with them, the more valuable the small chunks actually are."

As transcendentalist Henry David Thoreau wisely said, "The cost of a thing is the amount of life required to be exchanged for it." For Jordan, the price of endlessly chasing that next rung on the ladder wasn't worth exchanging his family time.

"If you are a dad who is gone sixty hours a week, your Saturday might be worth $3,000 to $5,000 if you're free to hang out with your kids," Jordan explains. "Sitting in the office waiting for a fax from a banker, which is what I used to do at the law firm on those weekends, barely seemed worth a fraction of that amount."

Jordan loves his work, but he also wants to be the dad who can say, *Let's go to Disney World!* on a Tuesday to avoid the long weekend lines. "I probably have a couple of years left where they still want to do stuff with me, and they aren't like, 'Dad is an old fart,'" Jordan jokes. Perhaps when that day comes, he can create those courses, go on that speaking tour, and write that book.

In the meantime, deciding to prioritize something other than the perpetual hustle doesn't mean he has to give back any of the trophies he's earned thus far.

You Don't Have to Give the Trophies Back

Sometime around early fall 2020, I stopped sleeping. It might have been the stress of trying to rebuild a travel-dependent, event-reliant, stage-centric speaking career in the midst of a pandemic that had decimated travel, shuttered events, and obliterated the stage. Perhaps it was the ever-growing pancake stack of tasks caused by working in the middle of a schoolroom or (depending on how you look at it) homeschooling in the middle of an office. Or maybe it was the night-sweat tidal waves heralding the unwanted beginnings of perimenopause.

More than a few of us stopped sleeping around that same time. So I assumed my sleep issue was your run-of-the-mill, everyday reaction to the corona-coaster we all collectively rode that year. I didn't know what was causing it—my guess was *(d) all of the above*—but it had been months since I had slept more than three hours a night.

When I don't get enough sleep, I cease to form intelligible words, let alone string those words together in a sentence. This presents a problem when your profession involves, say, writing books.

It wasn't just that I couldn't form words. I couldn't remember them either. And numbers? Forget about it. In the 0.8 seconds it took me to turn from the cookbook to the cabinets, I would forget how many teaspoons of sugar were supposed to go into my apple pie.

I was convinced that my brain was broken. I was sure that I was suffering through some sort of slow-motion, pandemic-related trauma, and that my brain was remapping itself in response. I like my brain, and I needed to form those pretty word-sentence things, so I sought professional help.

The shrink diagnosed me quickly (and quite correctly) with a case of the dreaded Overachiever Who Tallies Her Worth in Accolades disease. He put his pad down and said some rather profound words: "You know, Laura, you don't have to give the trophies back."

Possibly you, too, suffer from this same affliction. For years, you've plowed ahead, going from one trophy-acquiring project, program, or promotion to the next—never realizing the exertion, exhaustion, and enervation that this pace was drip-drip-dripping into your overachiever's veins. Suddenly, calamity hits (or perhaps you just encounter a minor bump in the road), and you're no longer able to muscle through work and home and life issues in your usual *Go Big or Go Home!* way.

"You've been operating at a pretty high level for a pretty long time. We can work on that if you'd like," the shrink offered.

"Work on being an overachiever, Doc? No, thanks," I demurred. "That's a feature, not a bug."

"How's your stress level?" he inquired.

"Seems fine to me," I countered.

"But . . . you're here," he checkmated.

It was hard to argue against his keen observations, his perfect personality profiling, *and* his blunt statement of the plainly obvious. I *was* there. And I had to face the fact that perhaps I needed to change my ways.

Yes, my brain was broken, but not in the way I thought. The pandemic had stopped me in my tracks, literally and metaphorically, forcing me to confront life's essentials now that I was no longer racing through airports, jostling onto shuttle buses, and hurrying into conference halls with my perfectly packed suitcase of awards and achievements. Without that giant suitcase full of trophies, I simply could no longer recognize myself.

That realization pushed me to start moving again, but at a completely different speed. Did I really need to crush it? Or could I stop for a while, sit down, breathe, rest?

That's exactly what I did. I stopped worrying about the trophies available for me to earn, and about reminding people of the trophies I already had. Those accolades weren't going anywhere—and neither was I, if I kept struggling, grinding to work harder and longer until I dropped.

Rather than focus on the long list of achievements I could collect, I took some time to focus on how I wanted to show up for the people I love: my friends, my family, my clients. I reminded myself to sit back for a while and just enjoy the ride.

This eventually got me moving again. And it turns out that it's a lot easier to move forward when you aren't clinging to those bulky, burdensome old trophies.

Remember Your Why

We live in a constantly connected, always-on, work-from-anywhere world, and it is making us sick.[1] And yet we ignore not only the symptoms (such as using our smartphones excessively and consulting articles with titles like *"Learn how high achievers can become even more productive!"*) but the cause: the misguided insistence that all this hustle is helping us create better work.

Have you ever been in the shower, or out on a leisurely run, or headed to school pickup, when you had the best idea ever? Have you ever woken up in the middle of the night with the perfect solution to a previously intractable problem? Have you ever been stymied by something complex, only to find it beautifully mapped out in your mind as soon as you stop thinking about it constantly? This is what happens when we let our brain rest. It's not that you do your best thinking in the shower; it's that the shower is the only place you actually stop to think.

Yes, you can always be working more. You can always be working harder. You can always be picking up more trophies. But should you? If you're too busy and too burdened to think straight, the answer might just be no.

Vinh Giang discovered magic when he was a young man and loved doing party tricks at the office. Over time, magic became more than a hobby. Performing tricks in the office turned into gigs during cocktail parties at conferences. Cocktail parties at conferences grew into main-stage keynotes. Soon, Vinh had conjured up a successful career, practically out of thin air. His parents were not thrilled. They had escaped war-torn Vietnam so their children could become doctors and lawyers. But Vinh was happy.

Except now he was constantly on the road, away from his wife and newborn son, doing a hundred gigs per year. He assumed the more he sacrificed, the more success he would have and the happier he would be. But what started off as a wellspring of joy and confidence was becoming a source of pain and insecurity. Vinh found himself in a deep depression, one that he refused to acknowledge. One gig felt the same as the next; he was starved for con-

1 Joshua Harwood et al., "Constantly Connected—The Effects of Smart-Devices on Mental Health," *Computers in Human Behavior*, 2014.

nection and impact. But he kept telling himself that he was lucky to be able to do this work—even though his burnout left him feeling anything but lucky.

One day, Vinh's father called to warn Vinh about losing track of his true desires, becoming too greedy, and being too focused on conquering. He worried that Vinh would be unable to sustain this pace. "A king who knows the limits to his desires will rule an entire lifetime," he said.

That one sentence made Vinh decide to stop traveling, move his family back home to Australia, and build a fully virtual training business. "I finally realized that I had it backwards: the more success, the more you had to sacrifice," he confesses. "And I was not willing to sacrifice anymore."

In a world obsessed with work, stepping away from the *bigger, better, faster, more* mentality can be scary. We are never promised an outcome, so we do what we know best: nose to the grindstone, shoulder to the wheel, just keep working. Resting on one's laurels is for the lazy, the elite, the unappreciative few who didn't earn their success, right? The other 99.9 percent of us needed to keep going, keep climbing, keep earning, right?

Nope.

You know what all this work, work, work does? It makes us too tired to enjoy the spoils of success. It takes us away from the reason we originally set out to do this work. It traps us in an unending cycle of having to outdo ourselves, when what we really need is a nap.

What's the point of "making it" if you don't actually enjoy what you've made? What if, instead of asking ourselves how much we could get, we asked ourselves how much is enough?

Saying *No, thanks* or *Not now* or *Nah, I'm good* goes against every rat-race milestone we're told that we are supposed to want. Yet every one of us can point to at least one person in our life who has substantially more money, more trophies, more stuff than we have, but who is substantially less happy. I wonder how often that person even stops to revisit the purpose of it all, or to remember what inspired them to start running that race in the first place.

Look closer at your purpose, and you just might find that the conventional wisdom—*keep growing, do more, build faster*—isn't the right wisdom for you. I'm not saying you should always be happy with where you are and what you have, especially if you are still reaching for specific goals. But remember periodically to look at your path, your pursuit, and your progress, and then decide whether you are still in the hunt for the right reasons.

Refocus on Your Passion

Leading up to each success, it's easy to get distracted by all sorts of trophies: the big job, the big salary, the big house, the big boat, not to mention the country club membership. But people who belong to that country club have even bigger jobs and bigger salaries and bigger houses and bigger boats. So, you redouble your efforts. You work harder, you get even more things, you outgrow your country club, and you join a bigger one where—guess what?—the toys are larger still.

You keep going and going, until you are working so hard that you never see the country club, other than an alert that pops up on the phone when your kids post pictures on Instagram from the pool.

Lucky them. Not so lucky you.

It's not your fault. This is a problem experienced by many, and a term was coined for it more than fifty years ago: *the hedonic treadmill.*[2] And it's the opposite of unwinding on a carefree, rejuvenating carousel ride.

As we make more money, we want more things, and as we get more things, we expect those things to bring us happiness . . . but they do not. Those things provide a temporary respite, but no permanent gain in our level of happiness. So, we jump back on the treadmill to make more, get more, and hope for that elusive permanent state of nirvana, which never comes.

Making your peace with Wonderhell often means stepping off that hedonic treadmill and changing your measure of success. The most conclusive, comprehensive way to make this change is by switching your metric from *how much you have* to *how many you can help.*

Over and over, successful people have told me that they avoided burnout by no longer pushing for achievement for themselves, for their own trophy

---

2 Philip Brickman and Donald Campbell, "Hedonic Relativism and Planning the Good Society," in *Adaptation-Level Theory*, ed. M. H. Appley (1971).

cases. Instead, they refocused their passion on those who count on them: friends, employees, fans and followers, family.

This shift in focus is what prompted Dr. Marshall Goldsmith to create the MG100, a collective of the top executive coaches in the world. It all started when Dr. Goldsmith, the number-one executive coach in the world, attended industrial designer Ayse Birsel's Design the Life You Love program and tried an exercise that would show him how he could do just that.

Ayse had asked participants to write down the names of their heroes. For Marshall, this list included Frances Hesselbein (former CEO of the Girl Scouts and recipient of the Presidential Medal of Freedom), Alan Mulally (former CEO of Ford Motor Company and Boeing Commercial Airplanes), Dr. Jim Kim (president of the World Bank), Peter Drucker (founder of modern management), Paul Hersey (noted behavioral scientist and a personal mentor of Marshall's), and Warren Bennis (organizational consultant and one of the world's greatest leadership thinkers). Then Ayse asked the group to describe what made them think of these individuals as heroes.

"I wrote that they were all great teachers and very generous," explains Marshall. "She then challenged us to be more like our heroes in designing the lives we love."

Marshall decided that he would teach everything he knew to one hundred students who were already carving a path of excellence for themselves as executives, authors, thought leaders, and coaches. He posted a video on LinkedIn, expecting to get a handful of applicants, and was surprised to get eighteen thousand responses. He chose the most interesting applicants, and challenged them to do exactly what he intended to do for them: teach others in their circle everything they knew, all in an effort to help as many high performers as possible perform at even higher levels.

For Marshall, this work wasn't an abrupt switch. He'd already been intentional with his time and his mentoring throughout his career, just as his mentors had been with him. He had good role models for this work, and he was a good role model, too. But his efforts at this stage represented a fuller acknowledgment that his measurement of success was not in the number of digits in his bank account, but in the number of lives he had changed for the better.

Marshall chose this new direction toward the end of a storied career, but we need not be in the twilight of our own career to shift toward what works for us. Vinh did it when he was in the middle of his career because he felt empty inside. And Rahaf Harfoush did it when her hair started to fall out.

Learning to Float

Rahaf Harfoush looked, from the outside, like a naturally successful person—completely at ease, totally in control, and unfazed by stress. Less obvious, though, was that just a few years ago, she had been unable to sleep, her soul riddled with anxiety and her scalp riddled with bald patches.

Rahaf had just finished a whirlwind book tour that resulted in lucrative consulting contracts, exciting media appearances, and a coveted spot on the *New York Times'* "Best-Seller List." And she didn't know what to do with herself next.

As she looked around for a project that intrigued her, her internet feed was assaulted over and over with productivity porn. *You're only as good as your next big idea* was something she'd read in several places, along with missives about how *very* successful people get up at 5 a.m. but the *most* successful people get up at 4 a.m. Everywhere she looked, the message was loud and clear: no matter how much she was doing, she wasn't doing enough.

One such message was even written on a white ceramic mug (and on hoodies, and on pillows, and on tote bags) with a picture of the Queen of Creative Productivity herself: *You have the same number of hours in a day as Beyoncé.*

Rahaf took the mug at face value. "Beyoncé has already done so much," she told her sister, Riwa. "I've wasted so much time being unproductive. My life is a failure." For Rahaf, though, this wasn't a shrug-your-shoulders surrender as much as a call to action.

She and Riwa decided to learn everything they could about what makes Beyoncé, well, Beyoncé. At first, it was disheartening, demoralizing, and downright depressing. Everything they read was focused on Beyoncé's unrelenting drive and indefatigable willingness to just keep putting in the work. She seemed to put as much energy into the aura of her work ethic as she put into the work itself. Really, where *did* she find the time?!

But then they found a small article, a barely-there mention, a whisper of a blip amid a sea of accolades and praise of a carefully managed public persona: between tours, in 2011, Beyoncé took a year off to focus on her mental health. As they dug deeper, they learned Beyoncé's mother had noticed that the megastar didn't always know what city she was in—that even while picking up trophies at awards shows, she was only thinking about her next performance. Rahaf recognized this trap.

We know what to do. We know how to take care of ourselves. We know what we need. We might even have the privilege and opportunity to change our ways. Yet we still don't take a moment's break until our hair starts to fall out.

Rahaf's next book, *Hustle and Float*, was born out of the questions she found bubbling up from within: Why do we know what we should do, but fail to do it? Why do we worship productivity and busyness as opposed to working toward specific, self-identified goals? And is all this hustle even getting us anywhere?

Rahaf took the book's title from whitewater rafting, where an optimal mix downriver includes plenty of hustle (navigating the rapids, making split-second decisions, paddling with all your might in intentional bursts of energy) but also just the right amount of float (pulling up your paddle and letting the river do the work for you).

Too much hustle, and you'll become exhausted, putting yourself and your teammates in peril as you make increasingly worse decisions with ever-reducing returns.

Too much float, and the trip gets pretty boring.

The best rafting trips involve a bit of both.

What Rahaf learned both surprised and relieved her. Hustle for hustle's sake is not only useless, but these ten-to-twelve-to-fifteen-hour days are actually making us *less* productive.

"Research shows that the real number of good, productive working hours per day is likely closer to six," she explains, drawing from all that she learned while developing her next book, aptly titled *Humane Productivity*. "After you spend six hours on a challenging mental task, your brain is basically done for the day. Staying later won't accomplish anything for you (or your boss). But it will push you toward your breaking point faster."

And this is where the float comes into play. Taking another leisurely trip on that merry-go-round is our opportunity to relax and reflect, make better decisions—and say no to the hustleporn attacking us from all sides.

ARE YOU READY FOR THIS RIDE?

Deep breaths, everyone. You don't always have to spin faster and faster in pursuit of bigger and bigger rewards. Sometimes the rewards you truly want—at your particular age and stage of life—are already right there in front of you. Sometimes the way you will thrive in this Wonderhell is by knowing you don't have to push forward to the next one quite yet.

You've collected the trophies, and you could keep striving, but there are advantages to choosing to slow down, too, especially if it allows you to focus more on the people, causes, and work you truly love.

Remember why you started. Remember what you wanted. When you're ready to start up again, all that you desire will be right there waiting for you.

As you decide whether to go peacefully around the Carousel again or jump to a new ride, consider the following questions:

- Are you pursuing the next big thing because you want it, or simply because it is there to be achieved?
- What are you sacrificing to achieve the next success, and is it worth it at this age and life stage?
- How can you use your success to impact other people in ways that will stave off burnout for you?

Focusing on What Matters

Everyone wants to leave the fairway a winner, and the Whack-A-Mole Game promises a big prize. But first you have to beat down the mechanical pests that pop up from their hidey-holes. *Pop! Pop! Pop!* As soon as you fix one problem, another appears. The bigger your life, the bigger your ego, the bigger your vision, the more distractions arise. Faster than you can swat them away, they *just . . . keep . . . coming.* Only by fine-tuning your priorities all along your ever-changing journey—to reflect what truly matters—can you produce your best work and find stability amid the insanity.

Figuring Out What Matters

Melissa Wiggins was on her own in the maternity wing of the hospital, giving birth to twins. Her husband was across the hospital bridge in the children's wing, holding their twenty-month-old son, Cannon, as he went through his first chemotherapy treatment. It was not how Melissa thought this day would go— not by a long shot.

Two weeks earlier she had noticed Cannon limping, and four days after that she learned that he had stage IV cancer. His scan showed tumors everywhere. "His body lit up like a Christmas tree," Melissa remembers. Their options were limited; most kids with that diagnosis don't make it. But Melissa, "a proud, stubborn, tough Scottish lassie," was determined to give her son's story a different ending.

Melissa's husband had a larger salary and better insurance, so they decided that Melissa should shut down her business and be available full time for what could be a years-long battle. Someone needed to be home, research various trials, find the right surgeons, and travel with Cannon to a range of medical centers. As Melissa and her husband figured out how to handle it all, they discovered something else: there were tons of other families just like theirs.

These other families, too, were facing overwhelming challenges, tackling urgent decisions, swatting down emergencies all day, every day. Should they choose radiation or go with surgery? Was it better to stay local or fly across the country to a top research institute? How could they keep their jobs, take care of their other kids, and even stay married?

Melissa was certain the answers were out there.

Cancer is the number-one killer of children—more common than every other reason added together—so finding all manner of nonprofits, from hair donations to vacation sponsorships, was no surprise. What did surprise Melissa was the lack of that one thing these families wanted most: more innovative research to keep their kids alive and well.

"All right, we'll try to make a difference," Melissa insisted. And the Cannonball Kids' cancer Foundation[1] was born.

What started as a labor of love, created while Melissa helped nurse Cannon into remission, became an international nonprofit that has delivered more than $3 million of innovative funding, advancing pediatric cancer research and gifting families more time with their children. Still, Melissa held a lot of little hands in dying days, consoled a lot of parents in their worst hours, attended a lot of devastating funerals. And the ambition to build something bigger, something more impactful, took a toll on her.

"I went too hard for a lot of years," Melissa says, thinking back on when she did the whole get-things-done-when-they-nap, after-bedtime, before-they-get-up thing. Cannon got better—and stayed better—but she was still

---

1 That's not a typo. It's a lowercase *c* because, as Melissa says, "cancer is undeserving of uppercase."

wrapped up in making a difference. "I did it, and I did it, and I did it, and then I hit a wall. I was completely burned out. I had no more 3 a.m.'s left."

So wrapped up in the tyranny of the urgent, the martyrdom of the busy, the suffering of other people's kids, she wasn't doing the most important thing of all. "I wasn't able to take my kids to school or pick them up. I wasn't able to be present for them," she explains. "I was failing my family, because Cannonball Kids' cancer Foundation always came first." Rather than building an institution that would outlive her, she was building a cathedral that existed only through her.

Although Melissa is a bit of a superhuman, alas, she is still human. Finally, she realized that she could make changes to her approach and still make a difference.

She started by making choices about what mattered most to her. Where could she really offer the most impact? What was the best use of her time? How could she reduce the stress and trauma and burnout of the calling that she'd found so unexpectedly? Figuring out how to take time for herself and her family was particularly difficult because, as she points out, "Cancer doesn't take a break."

In the end, Melissa determined which responsibilities absolutely had to be hers, and which could be shifted elsewhere by hiring staff and building a board of directors. In resolving the important questions and resetting her priorities, she found a new way to proceed. She stopped being so busy, and started being more focused on what mattered most to her: her family and even (from time to time!) herself.

Busy Is Bullshit

A common refrain as we travel through Wonderhell is, "I'm too busy."

I want to volunteer, but I'm too busy.

I want to work out, but I'm too busy.

I want to go back to school, but I'm too busy.

I want to be a better friend, but I'm too busy.

Are you really too busy? Or have you decided this is something that just doesn't matter that much, isn't the best use of your time, or doesn't rank high enough for you to prioritize?

We have a habit of overfilling our plates, whether because we are asked to manage more than we can handle, because we derive self-worth from being busy, or simply because everyone else is doing so. Then we seek out productivity hacks, up our caffeine consumption, work more and sleep less—and make excuses for not packing even more into our schedule. And the Toxic Positivity Army doesn't help, cheering us on as if we can bend the space-time continuum and promising, *You can do it all!*

That's bullshit.

I'm certainly not going to give you some trite pep talk about all the things you can accomplish daily, or brag about how I juggle it all simultaneously and with great poise. All who enter the "I'm Busier Than You" Cage Match of Death lose. To avoid this fight-to-the-certain-death, you must make a crucial decision: What really matters most to you?

We all prioritize, and when we do, we make time for our real goals. So, whenever anyone tells me, *I'm too busy*, here's what I really hear them say: *It's not that important to me.*

Don't have time to volunteer for that charitable cause? It doesn't matter to you that much.

Don't have time to train for that marathon? You aren't actually serious about it.

Don't have time to go back to school? You haven't really figured out what you're going to do once you earn that degree.

Don't have time to text someone back? You're just not that into them.

Perhaps that is harsh. But maybe, just maybe, it is liberating.

Former professional triathlete Travis McKenzie calls these goals—the ones you say you want but never actually prioritize—your "look-good goals." You know, the ones that look good on the vision board, look good to other people, look good on social media. But are those goals really important to *you?* Sure, they're fashionable, they're popular, they're pretty. But if you aren't putting them at the top of your to-do list, you don't really care about them.

And in pretending to pursue all of these goals, you likely will achieve none of them. The truth is that when you find yourself running *toward* what you want instead of running *away*, you will miraculously find the time. The stress will turn to excitement. The path will be paved with control and certainty. You will see a clear vision of your life the way you'd like it to be. And you will make it happen.

Be honest with yourself about what is and isn't standing in your way. And if you don't seem to ever make time for that look-good goal? That just frees you up for other things that matter to you more, giving you a chance to put those things first.

Eat the Frog Last

Productivity experts tell you to "eat the frog first." In other words, do the worst thing immediately, get it over with, and then move on to what truly matters. Oh, and do it first thing in the morning—the earlier, the better.

Entrepreneur whisperer Clay Hebert thinks this is bunk. He wants you to throw off the societal shackles of immediate responsiveness and workaholic devotion, and shift how you prioritize your time. "We always find time for the work that has to get done, but we do it at the expense of the things we love. What if we could do both?" he reasons. Instead of focusing only on strategies to make ourselves more *productive*, Clay wants us to be more *fulfilled*, too. He wants us to have the Perfect Calendar.

Clay's Perfect Calendar is built on a simple concept: The time we have—all 24 hours a day, 7 days a week, 365 days a year—is the container into which we must fit our lives, and we get to choose how we spend most of it. Why not spend your days in ways that work perfectly for you, filling your calendar with more of what matters to you and less of what doesn't?

Imagine taking control of when and how you spend your time. What activities do you want to prioritize? When do you do your best work? Who do you want to see? How much do you want to sleep? Start from scratch with an empty calendar, and then start adding in what you would consider to be a perfect day, week, month, even year. This becomes the template for how you schedule your time.

Let's say you are at your most creative in the morning after you've exercised, so you start by putting the *Exercise* and *Work* blocks in your calendar first.

Then you chunk off some time midday for *Lunch* and a little catch-up on whatever landed in your inbox that morning.

You allocate afternoons for *Meetings*, because your creative energy is lagging by then but your social energy is ready to be unleashed.

Now, when a request comes in for your time, you stop looking for any random open window, and instead choose an available slot that best fits the energy demanded of you. And you no longer squander your creative morning time in trying (and failing) to get to Inbox Zero.

Perhaps you aren't a morning person, though. If that's the case, here's a radical suggestion: just move your routine to later in the day. Turn that Miracle Morning into your own version: the Extraordinary Evening.

Can't get after it with the 5 a.m. club? Start a 5 p.m. club. What works for you is what works for you.

Grab Monday morning by the balls! Take Friday afternoon to the dance! After creating your Perfect Calendar for your typical, normal day, carve out all the other days—the ones that should be blessedly, fantastically, memory-makingly abnormal.

To better visualize this approach, Jesse Itzler (co-owner of the Atlanta Hawks, co-founder of Marquis Jet and ZICO Coconut Water, and author of *Living with a SEAL*) employs a Big Ass Calendar, so named because he literally carries one of those enormous paper wall calendars with him everywhere he goes. Even on airplanes.

The first thing Jesse does is make a list of the things he loves to do most. He picks adventures, schedules family trips, signs up for races. Then he grabs that Big Ass Calendar, and assigns dates and times to those events before anything else takes hold. He invites his friends and family so they can prioritize and protect this precious, fun-together time, too.

Whether your Big Ass Calendar is physically big or a normal-sized calendar (or maybe it's an app!), transitioning to your new, more perfect-for-you planning tool will take a bit of adjustment. You may need to shift your commute, reschedule a client, postpone a meeting, and replace that forty-minute presentation with a quick phone call. But you'll show up better and more energized for the things and people who matter to you most.

Now you have a plan, so you can protect your time before time passes you by—and decide when to eat your own damned frog.

Here's the next trick: operationalizing this blissfully perfect but still imaginary calendar in the real world, where clients, children, and chaos reign. That will require you to set some boundaries.

Set Boundaries

My assistant wrested control of my calendar from me after it became clear that time-zone math was my kryptonite. As a control freak who saw compulsively managing my calendar as a way to stave off the stress of Wonderhell, I was not happy about this. Our compromise was the calendar system described above, plus a nine-page document cheekily referred to as "How to Manage Your LGO." In that document, I set my boundaries.[2]

My algorithm goes something like this. (Yours will be different, naturally.)

First, I love to spend time with my kids, but I need (and actually also love) to spend time with my clients. And I travel almost weekly for work. So, I try to pick up my kids from school two days a week, if possible; three, if my work commitments allow; four, on a really good week. But never five. Let's face it: when it comes to teenagers, a cameo appearance beats a starring role.

When I do pick them up, I'm all theirs. I don't race back to the office. I'm not on calls. I'm just . . . around. Sure, they might grab a snack and squirrel it up to their rooms. (And I might answer a few of those remaining emails in my inbox. I'm still working on that addiction to immediate responsiveness, it seems.) But eventually they wander back downstairs—something to do with the siren song of dinner cooking on the stove—and then I can be there for them, present, available.

---

2 Really! Send me a message, and I'll share it with you so you can build your own.

Second, I don't meet and eat. Long ago, I noticed that all those morning or midafternoon meetings with people seeking to pick my brain led to lots of muffin eating and an ever-expanding muffin top. This was usually because such meetings come at the expense of a daily workout, which is, for many of us, the first personal commitment to be sacrificed.

And to be honest, the value of my advice (and the value of yours) is worth more than a $4.75 muffin. Don't get me wrong: for a big meeting with a big client, I'd saw off one of my limbs and eat it raw. But when someone just wants my casual opinion, I have thrown over the meet and eat for a much better (for both of us) meet and move.

It's not just better for us physically, either.

Our creativity, problem-solving ability, and general happiness improve while we're moving.[3] So, in addition to the physical benefits of meeting while on the move, there are mental benefits. As an added bonus, this approach roots out the tire kickers, showing me who is really serious and who is just spamming a ton of emails to a long, noncurated list. (For people who are not as mobile, I have also offered an option to make a donation in any amount to one of several charities I support, as a gesture of gratitude for my time.)

Third, and finally, I try to shove every single adulting-type meeting into the same day or two each week. I borrowed this strategy from Neil Pasricha, author of multiple best sellers, including *You Are Awesome: How to Navigate Change, Wrestle with Failure, and Live an Intentional Life*. Like the Perfect Calendar, his schedule includes "Untouchable Days," which hold windows of time that are most productive for his writing—three per week, which he blocks out far in advance. His genius hack: when necessary, shift these windows only to other days during the same week (but never to a different week). So when he has an inflexible commitment one morning, he simply moves that original block to another morning that week. That way, he doesn't lose out on a minute of the time he needs.

---

3 Marily Oppezzo and Daniel L. Schwartz, "Give Your Ideas Some Legs: The Positive Effect of Walking on Creative Thinking," *Journal of Experimental Psychology: Learning, Memory, and Cognition*, 2014.

As an added bonus, this method allows me to pre-plan my public-facing days and saves me from having to do the whole hair-and-makeup-and-hard-pants rigamarole every single day. I mean, really, who's got time for daily greasepaint and pointy shoes, anyway?

Perhaps that sounds trifling, but it's a legit concern. The average woman spends fifty-five minutes per day working on her appearance. That's two weeks per year! And it's not just women. Men are affected by this, too, spending an average of thirty-eight minutes per day polishing their looks.[4]

We do this because, consciously or subconsciously, we know that it matters. People who are rated as highly attractive, who "clean up good," earn 20 percent more than those considered to be only run-of-the-mill in terms of attractiveness.[5] I guess getting gussied up works. But that doesn't mean I have to like it, so I set my boundaries accordingly by limiting my makeup-and-hair days to one or two per week.

My time matters to me—and yours should, too. None of us can mold society into a more universally equitable place any more than we can add more time to Earth's revolution to suit our schedule. What you can do, however, is establish boundaries that will position you to focus on what matters most—and save the fake eyelashes for those rare, public-facing days when you need a bit of extra confidence.

The Entrepreneur's Journey

Ann McFerran wasn't always confident about how she acted or how she looked. And as a Thai immigrant who came to the United States with her single mother, knowing just a few words of English, she wasn't always confident about how she spoke. But she was always confident when she wore her fake eyelashes.

4 Melissa Dahl, "Stop Obsessing: Women Spend 2 Weeks a Year on Their Appearance, TODAY Survey Shows," Today.com, February 24, 2014, https://www.today.com/health/stop-obsessing-women-waste-2-weeks-year-their-appearance-today-2D12104866.
5 Jaclyn S. Wong and Andrew M. Penner, "Gender and the Returns to Attractiveness," Research in Social Stratification and Mobility, 2016.

For Ann, fake eyelashes were like a superhero's cape. She just wished the ones she could find on the market were better. And she knew she wasn't alone. The lash products that existed weren't great, and many people struggled to apply them. Why weren't there any *magnetic* lashes on the market? And where were all the super *glam* lashes she would've loved to wear?

"That's how I came up with the name Glamnetic," she reveals.

Ann began a process of research and development, drawing up plans for magnetic eyeliner and glamorous lashes with magnets attached. She contacted more than three hundred manufacturers to figure out how to create them. After a year's worth of trial and error and mailing samples all over the globe, her vision came to fruition. Glamnetic was real, and the lashes were starting to sell.

"My goal was just to make $10,000 a month, and I would have been happy," she says. "But the first month we did $20,000, and then the next month we did $40,000, and then $80,000, and then $160,000. It just kept doubling."

Ann was not expecting Glamnetic to grow so quickly. Like many entrepreneurs, she was doing all the things, all the time, carefully hedging her bets. She was building up her Instagram following, DM-ing with potential customers, shooting and editing all the photos and videos, ordering and stocking and shipping—all out of the bedroom of her tiny Koreatown apartment in Los Angeles, all while still working her day job.

By month six, Glamnetic was doing $1 million in sales monthly. Ann looked around her bedroom and realized that she needed a studio and maybe even an employee. She shouldn't be focused on packaging each lash and DM-ing with each customer.

Once again, Ann was moving fast. Each time she turned around—*pop! pop! pop!*—there was a new issue to manage. She quickly went from one employee to seventy, and this time, the challenge was new: How do you go from *doing* to *leading*?

Most professionals have a stopover on the journey, which usually goes from doer to manager to leader. But entrepreneurs don't always have this luxury. Ann had to do it all, all the time. She didn't have a moment to stop and learn the essential skills for the next level.

Ann thought about what she did best: act as the visionary and the face of the brand. But she also realized that she had to begin thinking about the culture of the company as a whole. So instead of leading every department—doing all the jobs and managing all the people—she promoted team leads for each department, who now would report to her.

"That's when everything changed," Ann says. "I can be more relaxed, knowing that if I don't show up to work one day, everything will be fine. Now my focus is on how I empower those team leads to do a better job."

Ann still takes part in all the meetings so she can remain aware of what's going on and help make key decisions, but her focus has shifted to what matters most to her, becoming a better leader. "The most important part of my job now," she says, "is 'How do I make people happy so they stay?'"

These days, a report of low morale would be more devastating to her than a bad sales report. Though with $50 million in sales in 2020 and her full focus on company culture, she probably doesn't get a whole lot of either type.

ARE YOU READY FOR THIS RIDE?

Any trip to Wonderhell would be incomplete without a million, billion, trillion things popping up, all of them screaming at equal speed and intensity: *Prioritize me! Prioritize me!* But should you?

As you peer into the future, straining toward your next Wonderhell, ask what matters most to *you*. You control your time and your to-do list, according to your priorities and your potential. To avoid overload and burnout, decide on the boundaries that will enhance your state of flow.

If you hit everything that pops up in this Whack-A-Mole Game, congratulations! You're surviving. But if you put down the mallet and stop aiming at every distraction . . . well, now you're *thriving*!

As you build out systems that will allow you to focus on what matters most, consider the following questions:

- What things (professional and personal) would you love to accomplish this year?

- When do you do your best work, and what sneaks onto your calendar during those times instead?
- What (and who) matters most to you?

Quieting Perfectionist Tendencies

★

Buckle up for the chaotic fun of the Bumper Cars—buzzing around, dodging each other, having a grand old time—until, *wham!* Out of nowhere, you get knocked off course. You haven't gotten this far without being a high achiever, someone who has the drive to succeed, and you probably have some perfectionist tendencies, too. That's a formula for extreme pressure and, if you don't learn how to handle it, an epic crash. Here's where you learn how to get back on track.

Replacing Perfectionism with Grace

Jonathan Fields discovered his grandfather's old set of paints when he was a teenager, and immediately built himself a workstation out of some old, stacked blocks and a door. He lost himself in each makeshift canvas, sometimes for days on end. It satisfied his impulse to create, and it felt good. He didn't have a name for this feeling at the time, but he now knows it as being "sparked."

"One of the components of being sparked is being able to access that state of flow when a sense of self merges with the activity, where you lose a sense of time," Jonathan says. "Everything either slows down profoundly or speeds up profoundly, and all those things started to happen to me."

At the time of his discovery, "Freaky" Fields (an unfortunate nick-name he picked up in the sixth grade) was experiencing the earliest throes of self-judgment and perfectionism. He would work for days and days painting album covers on jean jackets, and if the result wasn't exactly perfect—if it didn't match the vision he had in his mind (which was most of the time, because he hadn't yet developed his craft)—he would just trash it.

He wanted to be better, faster than he had any right to expect.

Jonathan's creative impulse battled with his expectations of perfec-tion. "I got brought to my knees a whole lot, knocked down a lot—plenty of moments where my standards have harmed me physically, emotionally, psy-chologically, and I think at some point you have to listen," he says. It would take decades of messing up, maturity, and meditation for him to find peace.

Meditation allowed Jonathan to balance his fascination for being sparked with a newfound understanding of grace: permission to let every-thing be as it needs to be, and acceptance of that as a temporary state, instead of thrashing and trashing what should be seen as a work in progress. This also allowed him to see himself as a work in progress, too.

Jonathan's fourth book, *Sparked*, pursues his fascination with what allows people to produce their best work. It debuted as an instant *USA Today* best seller, but Jonathan doesn't focus much on that. "In a weird way," he says, "what's more important to me is that there are sentences in this book I couldn't have writ-ten quite that way five years ago." He has now extended his time horizon of his expectations for himself. If it takes ten years to learn how to write a para-graph that really matches the vision in his head, he's okay with that.

Even as he settles into the notion of grace, the simple process of aging provides the gift of greater perspective. Older, wiser, broken, and rebuilt, Jona-than now experiences the art, design, music, and books of master craftspeople in a whole different way, and he has come to understand that what makes *him* different—even freaky—is also what makes him special. He now celebrates the way he sees the world, which leads to innovative ideas and approaches to his work. His unique worldview is his greatest asset.

No longer is life an urgent race against himself. Instead, Jonathan feels grat-itude for the opportunity to grow into something over time. When he unearths something that he wants to invest his time and energy in while developing the craft around it, he says to himself, *You know, I'm not there yet, and it will probably take me ten or fifteen years to get even close. But how cool that I have something to which I can devote myself for that window of time!* Even when he achieves that goal, only to discover a whole new threshold another ten or fifteen years down the road, he has learned to be less frustrated and more intrigued and inspired.

"It's not about perfectionism," he says, "but about showing up and being human. At the end of the day, I'm still Freaky Fields."

Perfectionism Is a Weakness

"Tell me about your weaknesses," I'd often ask job seekers during an interview. And without fail, the March of the Obvious Answers would begin.

"I tend to work too hard," was a perennial favorite.

"I sometimes get so focused I forget to leave work," was a reality stretch but still a regular.

And I could always count on the most usual of suspects, straight out of the *Job Seekers 101 Handbook*: "I am a bit of a perfectionist."

I would follow up and ask, "In what ways does that perfectionism harm you, and in what ways does it serve you?" Time and time again, this was a stumper for job seekers. Suddenly, their first answer seemed a bit less than, well, perfect. Perhaps this was because most didn't realize that there are actually three types of perfectionism.[1]

> *Self-oriented perfectionism* isn't so bad. It leads people to be conscientious and to maintain high performance standards; it is associated with work productivity and career success.
>
> *Other-oriented perfectionism* is associated with being judgmental and critical of other people's performance, holding them to exceptionally high standards, and micromanaging them to avoid mistakes—which often leads to strained relationships (especially at work).

---

1 Paul L. Hewitt et al., "The Multidimensional Perfectionism Scale: Reliability, Validity, and Psychometric Properties in Psychiatric Samples," *Psychological Assessment: A Journal of Consulting and Clinical Psychology*, 1991.

Socially prescribed perfectionism derives from a sense of pressure to be perfect in everything you do. This type of perfectionism is on the rise—not surprising in today's age of toxic social media, where our self-worth is tied up with unrealistic standards.

Having high standards is not, in and of itself, a bad thing. Self-oriented perfectionists use standards as a springboard to excel. Unfortunately, nearly half of perfectionists fall into one of the other two camps, and they pay the price for it.

No one wants to settle for mediocrity, for a life of less than what is right there for the taking. But striving for lofty goals founded on unhealthy perfectionism often produces higher levels of burnout, loneliness, stress, anxiety, workaholism, and depression. In fact, perfectionism has an overarching detrimental effect on both workers and their workplaces—and perfectionism and good performance are not even closely linked. Even if the perfectionist can achieve "perfect" results, the collateral damage outweighs the benefit.[2]

So, how do we manage our perfectionist tendencies? Start by asking whether your perfectionism springs from a drive toward achieving high standards for yourself, or from a fear of judgment, failure, or isolation from other people. If you are looking to thrill someone other than yourself—or constantly feeling that you are not good enough, fast enough, smart enough, [insert your anxiety here] enough—buckle up for an abrupt but necessary change in direction. It's time to let go of *perfect* and take hold of *deliberate practice* instead.

Make a Habit of Habits

At the height of the pandemic, I found myself losing track of the days, the weeks, the pounds. That was easy to do when Monday became Tuesday became Wednesday became Blursday—and when, by March 856th, pajamas were the last judgment-free zone left. Day in and day out, I was staring at my own face on videoconferences, until one day my cheekbones just flatout resigned.

---

2 Brian Swider et al., "The Pros and Cons of Perfectionism, According to Research," *Harvard Business Review*, 2018.

When was the last time I went for a jog? What even are shoes, anyway? Clearly, it was time to do something. But what?

For those of us chronic overachievers, often the answer is to set all manner of BHAGs—the bigger, hairier, and more audacious the goal, the better. So, I did. And then I sat on the sidelines as I failed at every single one.

Then I watched as my friends fail at their goals, too, and I realized we were all going about it the wrong way. We were seeking perfection, and beating ourselves up for falling even just a little bit short. We were setting aspirational goals when we really should have been creating a deliberate practice of effective habits.

"We are what we repeatedly do," said historian Will Durant, interpreting Aristotle in *The Story of Philosophy*. "Excellence is not an act, therefore, but a habit." And no, you don't need to put in ten thousand hours to *perfect* the thing before you *do* the thing. You can just ... start! And instead of setting your sights on the highest (and most unattainable) bar possible, start small, aim low, and go slow.

Yeah, baby, you read that right! Look at the floor. Can you see your goals all the way down there? If so, they are too high. I'm not just talking floor or basement. I'm talking sub-basement ... cellar ... hidden room under the foundation.

Want to lose a hundred pounds? Lose just one pound this week.

Want to run an ultramarathon? Walk for ten minutes today.

Want to become a confident dancer? Do a two-step in front of your dog.

We have to start out somewhere, but the inflexible pursuit of perfection paves the road with potholes and tire-spikes. If we set "the new normal" as perfection and perfection alone, the minute we fall off the wagon, we lose all progress, labeling ourselves complete and utter failures and packing it in until December 31, when the magic of a New Year's resolution will, at long last, finally set us free.

I don't know about you, but I've had way too many sugar-free New Year's resolutions upended by those wonderfully fiendish young entrepreneurs known as Girl Scouts. So, I know two things to be true.

First: if eating an entire sleeve of Thin Mints is wrong, I don't want to be right.

And second: starting small, aiming low, and going slow allows you to be deliberate rather than just aspirational.

Anders Ericsson describes this practice in *Peak: How All of Us Can Achieve Extraordinary Things*. It starts with finding an intrinsic drive toward something you actually want (not something you've been told you want). Then, Ericsson recommends creating specific and measurable goals by breaking down your BHAG into smaller, bite-sized actionable steps, each of which is easily attainable. From there, he asks us to commit one hour a day to these goals, set up systems of feedback to measure improvement each day, and make sure we rest so we come back fresh to the next session.

As for me and my poundemic pajamas, I nerded out and built a spreadsheet to track nutrition, hydration, movement, and sleep—the pillars of any healthy lifestyle.

I followed a specific diet of tracking my macros, although I could just as well have chosen paleo, keto, vegan, Mediterranean, or any other system.

I drank a gallon of water a day.

I moved sixty minutes each morning, whether it was weightlifting, running, rowing, or yoga—choosing a workout as intense or restorative as I needed.

And I aimed to sleep eight hours a night.

But life can get crazy and sometimes feel out of control, especially (but not exclusively) in the middle of a pandemic. So, I took a different tack from my normal all-or-none, self-harming perfectionism: I gave myself partial credit.

Following that advice about bite-size steps, I assigned four points to each section of my spreadsheet. If I followed the nutritional plan for the whole day, that was four points. Yay me! Three-quarters of a gallon of water was three points, not four. Still, yay me! Likewise, a half-hour of movement (not a full hour) got two points. Six hours of sleep (not eight) earned three points.

Any day with an average over three points for each section was a win.

Yay me! Yay me! Yay me!

The most important part of the spreadsheet, however, was the final two columns: *What worked well today* and *What to focus on tomorrow*. The notes I scrawled in those columns each day gave me not only the satisfaction of meeting certain standards, but also permission to be imperfect and yet deliberate in my habits, because tomorrow is a new day. (And it's a day free of Thin Mints because—*burp!*—they are all gone. Problem-solving, FTW!)

It was a formula geared to the habits of perfectionists, not perfectionism itself. Each mini-achievement was a corrective, cumulative step toward success. The tenacity to pick yourself up, recover from failure, and restart as many times as necessary—grit—is what turns you into the person you have resolved to become. And that goes not only for you and me but for those people we elevate onto pedestals as well.

It's Okay to Not Be Okay

Fear. Uncertainty. Isolation. Doubt. Anxiety. These are not emotions that we expect to feel when we reach the highest pedestal of success. Yet they happen to the best of us.

What if you are in a role where perfection is expected, where it's a given?

Leaders are supposed to have all the answers.

Busy people get shit done.

Success means not having any problems.

If that's what you've always thought, you'll be surprised to find out Michael Phelps had the same problems as the rest of us. It turns out that we all get knocked about by the Bumper Cars.

When fifteen-year-old Phelps told a reporter he'd maybe like to compete in multiple Olympic events, he could never have known that his name would become synonymous with the sport of swimming, or that he would become the most decorated Olympian of all time. Nor could he have known the toll it would take on his mental health.

The pressure to be the best is at the core of high-level competition, and it's who Phelps was since he was eleven years old. But when he retired from swimming after the 2016 Olympic Games in Rio de Janeiro, he didn't feel like the best. Quite the opposite.

For two decades, his prowess—and his sacrifices—grew and grew. At each Olympic Games, he succeeded. At each Olympic Games, he wanted more. At each Olympic Games, he fought the demons inside that demanded perfection.

"If your whole life was about building up to one race, one performance, one event, how does that sustain what comes after?" Phelps asks. "Sure, go back to the grind, but that doesn't sustain. There was one question that hit me like a ton of bricks: Who was I outside of the swimming pool?"

And he wasn't alone.

In his film *The Weight of Gold*, Phelps documents the stories of Olympians Apolo Anton Ohno, Sasha Cohen, Gracie Gold, Jeremy Bloom, Shaun White, Lolo Jones, Bode Miller, and Katie Uhlaender, all of whom managed to find their way out of their darkness. The documentary also follows Olympians Steven Holcomb, Jeret "Speedy" Peterson, Stephen Scherer, and Kelly Catlin, who did not.

Showing promise at a young age, each of these accomplished phenoms imagined they could one day make it to the Olympics. None had a normal childhood. Instead, they sacrificed family, friends, relationships, school, work, and anything else that wasn't directly connected to helping them win.

"It's gold," says Ohno, a speed skater, "and . . . what?"

No one remembers the name of the person who comes in second, yet the difference between first and fourth place is microseconds, he explains. That leaves these athletes to spend years or even decades thinking about what will close the gap: *Just one more time around the track . . . one more lap in the pool . . . one more session in the weight room . . .*

Each of the smiling athletes we see marching in the opening ceremonies got to the Olympic Games because of that ability to hyperfocus, yet at the end of the day, they are just regular folks. Whether they won gold or not, every athlete was still left in their darkness and solitude, wondering, *What now?*

We are all perfectionist overachievers to some degree, trained to believe we can make ourselves unbeatable if we just keep working at it. Like high-performing athletes, our work is often solitary and dependent only on ourselves, which leads us to the self-fulfilling conviction that in no way should we ever need help. Our inner monologue, like theirs, stokes the fear that showing any vulnerability will make us weak. Olympians are trained to keep their pain out of sight, to focus on performance, to never show weakness—just like me and you and so many other high performers outside of the athletic arena.

"I won a shit ton of medals, but it didn't matter. I had no self-love. I had no self-worth," Phelps concludes. He finally managed to get off that unforgiving treadmill to nowhere and quiet that harmful perfectionism for good. Now he wants the world to know: "It's okay not to be okay."

Just Do One Run, and See How You Feel

Alex Ferreira is one of the most accomplished athletes in one of the most dangerous sports in the world: freestyle skiing. He knows all about perfectionist tendencies.

Growing up in Aspen, Colorado, home of the world-class X Games, Alex learned to ski practically before he learned to walk. "We used to skip out on middle school and take the bus over to the X Games just to watch some of the guys or girls practicing," Alex admits. "We were addicted."

As a young athlete, he began to show promise, but he also started having nightmares about being top-ranked in the competition but falling on a crucial run and blowing his shot at the big win. And when the time came for Alex to actually compete, he didn't know if he would be ready.

His solution was to outwork everybody. His solution was to be absolutely perfect.

And it worked.

From 2014 until 2019, he stood on podium after podium, on some of the biggest stages in his sport: the X Games, the Dew Tour, the Olympics.

In a sport as young as freestyle skiing, you're inventing it as you're competing in it. The impossible remains so only until someone goes out and does it. Alex's twists and turns and flips as he sails through the air are akin to Roger Bannister's four-minute mile: no one thinks it can be done until someone does it—and then it suddenly becomes possible for everyone else, too. That meant Alex had to keep getting even better.

He had to keep outworking the competition. He had to become even more perfect.

And he did.

"It was insane," he recalls. "It was the most money I'd ever made, the happiest I'd ever been, the most people wanting to be around me. It was just a glowing period in my life, for sure."

When the 2019 season ended, though, the cheering died down, the people went away, and Alex became depressed. For this happy, charismatic, optimistic adventurer, feeling that way would normally be difficult to understand. On the heels of the accolades, the financial status, the family and friends, and everything he'd achieved, it was completely mystifying.

He knew he was better than that. But he didn't know how to find his way back to being perfect.

So he did nothing at all.

After a summer of traveling, not training or working out, and just kind of finding himself, twenty-five-year-old Alex woke up one day realizing it was September—three full months later than when he usually started training for the X Games, which offered the biggest prize in his sport and was the one competition where he had not yet won gold.

He got back to work on seeking perfection—back on the skis, back in the weight room, back on the trampoline. And then one afternoon before the start of training camp, Alex threw his back out.

He was not going to be perfect.

Alex thought he would have to pull out of the X Games. "I just felt horrible, absolutely horrible," he recalls about that day of the competition. "I was using every ounce of energy just to walk to the top of the halfpipe."

"Just do one run, and see how you feel," his coach urged. "And then you can leave after that."

When his turn came, Alex was far from perfect. But he managed that first run, and a lifetime of good habits, determination, and pure love of the sport pushed him to try another, and another. He even fell on his last run, just like in his childhood nightmares. But his other runs were good enough to snag that big win he'd wanted his entire life.

I freaking did it! I won gold! Alex thought. *I've been thinking about this since I was ten years old, and I cannot believe I'm on top of the box right now.*

Pretty good for a guy who was thinking about withdrawing just twenty minutes before the competition because he couldn't possibly be perfect.

ARE YOU READY FOR THIS RIDE?

You have one life, and almost no one complains that it's too long. But all-out pursuit of a goal at the cost of everything else leads to burnout, exhaustion, depression, or worse. So, either you can accept the pressure to do everything instantaneously (and flawlessly!), or you can pursue your passion while also taking care of yourself—and taking time to enjoy life, too.

When perfectionism knocks you off track, remember the lessons of the Bumper Cars. Take each fender-bender in stride and adjust to a speed that works for you. Give yourself a break! Those bumps in the road can even be fun—and they bring perspective, confidence, and a fuller appreciation of all that awaits you down the road.

As you think about how to manage your perfectionist tendencies, consider the following questions:

- In what ways does perfectionism harm you, and in what ways does it serve you?
- What small habits can you put into deliberate practice that will help you achieve bigger results over time, in a more humane way?
- What would you lose if you weren't always perfect, if you asked for help, if you didn't have all the answers—and what would you gain?

Standing Tall When the Floor Drops Out

★

A little bump along the way is one thing, but what happens when crisis hits and the floor completely drops out from underneath you? That's exactly what you'll experience on the Gravitron, where disaster and panic reign at nauseating speeds. You'll be damaged! You'll be diminished! You'll be destabilized! And, you'll learn how crisis brings clarity, forcing you to recognize, accept, and even capitalize on your new reality—so you can face whatever comes next.

The Standards Don't Change

Joe De Sena likes to do burpees. And he wants you to like them too.

What's a burpee? It's a hellacious combination of a push-up and a jump on infinite repeat, lighting your whole body on fire and dredging up nausea from your belly, until you wonder if what's about to come up is a burp . . . or worse.

In the Spartan Race—the world's leading obstacle course competition, founded by Joe on his farm in Vermont—burpees are a form of punishment. You can skip an obstacle, but you must do ten, twenty, even thirty burpees, depending on the difficulty of that obstacle. Why? Because the standards don't change. If you are supposed to do a hard thing, you do a hard thing.

In Spartan's early days, it was fun for Joe to think about changing a bunch of lives. "Let's put on a really cool event," was the entirety of his plan back then. At first, seven hundred people showed up. Then fifteen hundred. Then three thousand. Joe was hooked, and he wondered if he could do even more.

He knew it would be hard. "There's gonna be rough seas, and we're gonna hate each other sometimes," Joe explained to his team. "We're gonna question our existence and why we're doing this. But our mission is to change one hundred million lives."

Heading into 2020, Spartan was on its way to achieving that goal, hosting three hundred events in forty-five countries and engaging more than seven million people. Then COVID-19 brought Spartan to an immediate, overnight, screeching halt. Joe was faced with figuring out how to uphold the high standards that the Spartan community had come to expect from him, while in the middle of an existential crisis that threatened to demolish the business he'd spent ten years building.

With Joe, the answer is always simple, obvious, and devoid of excuses. "I remember on that first day of lockdown, thinking, 'The standards don't change,'" he says. "We woke up early before the lockdown; we're going to wake up even earlier now. We put on clothes and went to work before; we aren't going to just walk around the house wearing pajamas all day now.'"

Sure, the bottom had dropped out. Everything he'd achieved in the past decade had fallen apart, but like with those damned burpees, he couldn't just quit.

"If we are going to transform one hundred million lives," Joe says, "we aren't going to do that sitting on the couch." He decided right away that just treading water wasn't enough.

Instead, he went even harder, instigating daily videoconference calls with his Spartan community—doing workouts together four times a day, every single day. "You've got to experience hard," he told everyone, "and then you've got to practice adversity."

There were some dark moments when Joe wanted to quit. But then he'd get an email from someone, sharing how much it meant to them that he just kept showing up, over and over. Plus, Joe knew he'd be much happier with himself if he could look back and say, *I spent the pandemic bingeing on workouts*, rather than *I spent the pandemic finding the end of Netflix.*[1]

Even though Spartan is now running races all over the world once again, Joe still has those dark, painful moments when he thinks, *What the hell am I doing? This business sucks!* But then he gets back to that purpose and reminds himself, *Wait a minute, we are going to change one hundred million lives.* And he waits for another email to arrive from someone whose life was changed by Spartan.

And then he thinks, *All right. I have another day in me. And the standards will be just as high tomorrow as they are today.*

We Are the Problem

Joe certainly isn't alone in his experience. Things changed for many of us when the threat of the pandemic made the world suddenly unrecognizable. Over just a few weeks, we went from business as usual to wondering whether we should sanitize our groceries, let the sunshine disinfect our mail, and hoard that last roll of two-ply at the local market.

We were trying to adjust to the new normal, not just at home but at work, too. For Joe, managing this upheaval meant showing up on video calls and doing burpees four times a day, for months on end. For me, it meant fielding email after email that made it clear my nascent public speaking career was taking a nosedive.

The arrival of COVID-19 grounded the travel sector and decimated the events industry. The stages where I'd been making my living were all hanging out their CLOSED UNTIL FURTHER NOTICE signs. And for the first few months of the pandemic shutdown, I whined and cried to anyone who would listen. COVID-19 was the problem. COVID-19 was not letting me get on planes and stages. COVID-19 was killing the motivational speaking business that I'd spent the previous four years building. I was pissed.

---

1 No disrespect to the Tiger King. (And while people rarely agree on anything, I think we can all agree that Carole Baskin *definitely* killed her husband.)

My frustration came out in many forms. I got political, blaming elected officials who I felt were favoring political expediency over science. I got personal, blaming neighbors who I suspected weren't washing their hands enough or staying at home. I got judgmental, blaming people who seemed to be choosing immediate, personal gratification—by insisting on flying, cruising, and spring-breaking—over the common good.

None of it changed the outcome. Chaos reigned, and my business tanked.

I wanted someone to blame for the floor dropping out, so I blamed everyone I could think of. Except it wasn't their fault. It wasn't even COVID-19's fault. It was mine.

As it turns out, *I* was the problem.

During my pity party—as I mainlined s'more after s'more after s'more, melted over the burning ashes of a business that had screeched from warp speed to snail's pace—I had a moment of clarity. COVID-19 wasn't stopping me from doing what I love, with people I love. COVID-19 wasn't stopping me from helping people get unstuck and live limitless lives. I was stopping myself.

I was the problem, because I believed the only way to do my job was how I'd always done my job.

I was the problem, because I assumed that stages and audiences come in only one form.

I was the problem, because I decided—with no basis in fact—that I couldn't possibly reach an audience bigger than an auditorium full of people, and that without those people staring right at me, hanging on my every word (hey, a girl can dream!), I couldn't make an impact.

Each of us chooses our path, and we may feel absolutely certain about it—until chaos strikes and flings everything up in the air. What if, instead of letting chaos stop us in our tracks, we allowed it to redefine our "stage" and expand beyond what we previously thought possible? What if whatever shakeup you are facing right now is offering you a chance to show up in new and different ways that add to whatever makes you special? What if you could completely reimagine your work, so you could be even better for the people you love and the causes you hold dear?

Sure, COVID-19 upended the way we worked, led our teams, and organized our communities. It was a difficult and frightening experience, but for all we lost, we also found ourselves open to new possibilities.

When I stepped back from the panic of uncertainty and saw things in the light of opportunity, I realized: *When else has access to other people's minds, hearts, and wallets been so democratized? What is stopping me from offering the solutions I can offer, other than my preconceived notions of what my stage should look like?*

I finally understood: there was a whole new amusement park in town. Courses! Virtual keynotes! Coaching! And the humble price of entry was nothing more than a webcam and an internet connection.

When the bottom fell out, I was paralyzed by doubt and indecision—until I sought a way forward, even if imperfect, toward an even better new normal. Once I stopped looking elsewhere for something to blame, I realized the true problem was my own response to crisis: my lack of clarity and creativity.

We might be the problem, but we can also be the solution.

We just need to transform our truth.

Transform Your Truth

Look, the truth is scary. Being seen is scary. There is doubt and uncertainty and, *eek*, shame in those hills. But they also might just be the key to everything that you want to unlock inside of you.

Researcher Brené Brown spent six years researching shame, with thousands of stories, and hundreds of interviews, to determine what gives people a sense of worthiness, love, and belonging. In her wildly popular TEDx talk, she described that "the people who felt worthy of love had courage, and could tell the stories of themselves with the whole of their hearts. They had the courage to be imperfect. Compassion to be kind to themselves first. They had connection as a result of authenticity. They were willing to let go of who they thought they should be, and were able to be who they actually were."

What if you could use this vulnerability as a super power to guide you through Wonderhell to a new, more meaningful truth? Amberly Lago, Orlando Bowen, and Samra Zafar did just that.

When an SUV hit Amberly's motorcycle, it took away her successful career, and it threatened to take her leg, too. She had made a good living in the fitness and modeling industries; her strong, athletic legs brought her both a paycheck and an identity. Now everything was spiraling out of control—but she held on. She wasn't about to let the doctors amputate unnecessarily. Thirty-five surgeries later, Amberly still has what she calls her "crumpled, disfigured leg"—only now that leg is a source of pride, of truth, and of a new identity as she travels the globe, teaching others how to manage pain, loss, and despair.

When Orlando was racially profiled, then pulled over and beaten by the police—who were later accused of planting drugs in his car to excuse their crime—it ended his career as a professional football player in Canada. One of the police officers served jail time for drug trafficking,[2] but there was never even a public admission of wrongdoing. The flagrant injustice was enough to conquer anyone's spirit, and Orlando originally had no interest in forgiveness, grace, or understanding. But owning his truth, and accepting that his life had taken a different path, led him to found the One Voice One Team youth foundation to inspire kids and teach them resilience, leadership, and teamwork.

When Samra was married off at age sixteen, taken to another country, and enslaved in her own home for ten years, she wasn't thinking about becoming an international advocate on behalf of child brides. But that was her truth, and once she understood that her situation was not normal and discovered a world outside of her own, she knew she had to stand strong. Now she is pursuing a medical degree so she might work in public health, helping other women and girls to escape living in the hell she once endured.

---

2 Gordon Paul, "Convicted Police Officer Sheldon Cook Gets Out of Prison after Serving One-Sixth of Sentence," *The Record*, October 30, 2105, https://www.therecord.com/news/waterloo-region/2015/10/30/convicted-police-officer-sheldon-cook-gets-out-of-prison-after-serving-one-sixth-of-sentence.html.

How did Amberly, Orlando, and Samra find a future amid their darkest moments, when happiness and accomplishment seemed forever out of reach? By coming to terms with the fact that the life they imagined for themselves was not the life they were going to live now.

None of them had a choice. But each of them found opportunity in disaster.

Each had to let go of emotions—bitterness, hate, anger, grief—that were eating them alive. Because regardless of whether the painful moment is instantaneous (as for Amberly or Orlando) or your life is eroding beneath you over time (as for Samra), one thing is certain: holding on to *who you were* will swallow you whole if you don't find a way to focus on *who you will choose to become*.

Amberly, Orlando, and Samra each had different circumstances, but the questions facing them were the same. Would they continue to live begrudgingly in the world forced upon them, spinning in an endless cycle of misery, blame, and self-pity? Or would they own their story, let people see the scars, and create a new life that was even more meaningful than they imagined?

If things have gone sideways for you, you might recognize this dilemma. In the grip of terrible pain, it can be easier to spend your days hiding in shame, making up stories, pointing fingers, justifying your actions, and denying what has happened. Or, you could choose to own the story, to be vulnerable and imperfect, to know that growth often comes through the most unwelcome of circumstances, and to let this new reality show you that a different life is possible.

This acceptance of your new reality isn't just giving up. It's quite the opposite. It allows you to take the knowledge, network, and resources you've gathered up to this point and channel them toward where you could go next. It is intrinsic to expanding your view of what else is even possible for you. And, it starts by fully embracing the vulnerability. As Brené learned, the difference was "the belief that what makes us vulnerable is also what makes us beautiful."

"It comes down to letting ourselves be seen, deeply seen, to love with our whole hearts, to practice gratitude and joy in those moments of terror, and to believe that we are enough," she explains.

And that means making a fundamental shift in the question you ask yourself.

What, Not Why

When something unexpected or even dreadful happens, often our first reaction is to ask: *Why me?* But what if, instead, we chose to ask a more practical, meaningful question: *What next?*

"Asking 'why?' is not useful," says Dr. Tasha Eurich, author of the *New York Times* best seller *Insight: The Surprising Truth About How Others See Us, How We See Ourselves, and Why the Answers Matter More Than We Think*, and the world's leading expert on self-awareness. "It's widely assumed that introspection—examining the causes of our own thoughts, feelings, and behaviors—improves self-awareness," she explains in her TEDx talk, which has racked up four million views and counting. "Yet one of the most surprising findings of our research is that people who introspect are *less* self-aware and report worse job satisfaction and well-being."

She explains the reason *Why?* is a surprisingly ineffective question to help us reach self-awareness: We don't have access to all the thoughts, emotions, and motives in play during our decision-making that led us to our current problem state. We think our brains operate like rational, objective computers, but truthfully we are irrational beings. We grab hold of something we are certain is right, and then we search high and low for "facts" that confirm this assumption, whether or not those facts are relevant or even true.

Why questions trap us in that rearview mirror, focusing only on ourselves and the cause of our misery: *Why did this terrible thing happen? Why aren't things working like they used to?* Sure, these questions can add context to our situation, like pointing out that someone is trying to hurt you because he is in pain himself, or that your boss was short-tempered with you after fighting with her spouse. But asking *why* something happened looks backward; it doesn't form a path forward. In fact, asking *why* leads us into a state of self-pity, depression, and anxiety—and few good decisions on a path forward are ever made from there.

So instead of asking *why* questions, Tasha suggests we consider *what* questions instead.

What questions focus us on what we can control and move us toward a brand-new future. "Asking 'what' gives us a plan of action," Tasha says, "and can help us stay objective, future-focused. It empowers us to act on our new insights."

Something transformative happens when you stop asking, *Why me?* and start asking bolder, more valuable questions: *What can I do next? What do I want to become? What change do I want to make in the world?* And this bold new approach can change what looked like hell into a new path of wonder.

For Amberly, Orlando, and Samra, *What?* questions like these led to speaking their newfound power to the world—open, raw, vulnerable, and honest.

Amberly accepted that things in her life are imperfect, and asked, "What happens now?" Her social media feed now prominently displays her leg to inspire others to also embrace their scars.

Orlando admitted that his athletic prowess was no longer his defining feature. He let himself be vulnerable and asked, "What good can come from my experience?" That's how he found a way forward, and now he teaches that path of forgiveness.

For Samra, asking for help from the health center at her university was the scariest thing she ever did, but it allowed her to find her voice. She asked, "What can I do to make a difference?" and now uses that voice to save other women in situations like hers.

Each of their decisions to open up fully to the unvarnished truth of their lives is a type of strength that we can all use on our own journey. By facing our catastrophic moments head-on, we can prove to ourselves and the world just how rewarding an unexpected path can be.

Death Has Interesting Things to Say

Jackie Summers was never one to let the *circumstance* distract from the *solution.* And the circumstance, in this case, was a golf ball–sized tumor in his spine.

The surgery sounded complicated—spinal cord this, nerve damage that. Jackie walked out of the appointment knowing three things for sure.

One, he had a 50/50 chance of coming out of this complex surgery paralyzed.

Two, he'd need to get his affairs in order, in case the cancer had spread to his lymphatic system.

And three, before going under the knife, he was going to go on the best vacation of all time.

"I didn't expect to survive," he explains. So, he got his nine closest friends together and rented a beach house in Cancun, with good food and good conversation and good booze.

He awoke one morning before everyone else and decided to grab a bottle of mezcal and take a walk on the beach alone. While strolling along the shoreline, Jackie thought about his life—five years on Wall Street, ten years as an advertising executive, another ten years as a publishing executive—always shoehorning himself into companies that neither suited him nor welcomed him as a Black man.

It was time to reassess his priorities.

Death, walking at his side, said, "So, I've finally got your attention."

Jackie decided that if he survived the surgery, he was going to drink for a living.

"The interesting thing about making your peace with Death," he says, "is that you can't unmake it." When he woke up from surgery and heard the word *benign*, he knew what he had to do.

Jackie asked himself again if he really wanted to drink for a living, and the answer was a resounding, *Yes!* "I wanted to be around cool-ass people in the middle of the day, in the middle of the week," he says, "talking about shit that matters, having good food and good conversation and good booze. And I wanted to monetize it."

He was ready to make lemonade out of lemons—or more accurately, demonade out of demons. But who would pay him to do this?

Jackie's roots are Caribbean, and so is the family recipe that he'd always made in his kitchen. Known as sorrel, it contains hibiscus flowers boiled with added spices and rum—and it is delicious. Even though it had been around for more than four hundred years, no one had ever bottled it. After decades of struggle in corporate America, Jackie decided it would be easier to start his own liquor brand than to go that old shoehorn route again.

He couldn't let his family history be swallowed up by some corporate entity. He had to do it himself.

Doing that meant getting a license to make liquor, something no Black person in America had done since Prohibition. Little did Jackie know how hard it would be—next to impossible, as it turns out. "But it also turns out that next-to-impossible things are kind of my schtick," he laughs.

The process was designed to be prohibitive. "It's a ten-year background check—everywhere you've worked, everywhere you've lived, every dime you've made, federal, state, and city," Jackie explains. "Plus, they expect you to pay rent on an empty space while you're waiting to be approved. They expect you to buy all this equipment—hundreds of thousands of dollars' worth—and put it in this space, not making a dime while you wait."

And that process can take up to two years.

But Jackie did it. After hundreds of failed attempts at perfecting the recipe, his brand Sorel was finally born. And in 2022, it swept awards in nearly every industry category, including the Chairman's Trophy in the Ultimate Spirits Challenge, Best in Show in the Great American Spirits Competition, and Best American Herbal Liqueur in the World Liqueur Awards.

Now, Jackie is convinced that being aware of life's fragility is the key to making the most of the time we're given. And when he thinks back on the path he thought life would take—and the path Death took him on instead—he wonders if the floor dropping out maybe wasn't such a bad thing.

ARE YOU READY FOR THIS RIDE?

It's all fun and games in Wonderhell until the bottom drops out, and suddenly you are pinned to the walls of the Gravitron with nothing but the force of momentum to keep you going. It's terrifying, but it's also clarifying. Crisis can reveal what truly matters, giving rise to a sense of purpose beyond your normal, everyday ambitions. Although your world seems to be ending, a new world awaits you on the other side.

Don't hesitate to ask, *Why me?* Instead ask boldly, *What next?* That way lies creativity, opportunity, and adventure.

As you try to regain your footing, get from crisis to clarity, and strike out on the path ahead, consider the following questions:

- How have you been holding on to blame, self-pity, or the status quo, and how might you approach problem-solving differently if you released yourself from those bonds?
- What must you accept about your new reality in order to move forward?
- What would happen if you asked yourself fewer *why* questions and more *what* questions?

Adopting a Beginner's Mindset

★

You might be tempted to hold on to where you've already been, but that will slowly steal your wonder and leave you with nothing but the hell. Lucky for you, the Loop-de-Loop is filled with unexpected twists and turns, ready to flip you upside down and inside out as you whirl through each corkscrew turn. You'll coil away from the familiar and hurtle into the unknown—around and around, in countless cycles of topsy-turvy growth and self-discovery, until you don't even know where you are anymore. So remember: every success (like every crisis) brings a new opportunity to rewind, recalibrate, and restart from the bottom up, so you can find your next Wonderhell.

The Magic Is in the Red Ink

Antonio Neves was on autopilot, and that got him fired.

He'd arrived in New York City just two and a half years earlier, with $800 in his bank account and dreams of working in the television industry—dreams that came true, for a while. No one who knew Antonio growing up would have predicted success anyway. Before graduating from high school, he'd moved more than fifteen times in his small Midwestern hometown. His mother and his father counted a total of six divorces between them. For a while, he lived in a shelter for battered and abused women and children.

So, he knows what it's like to have to start over.

Antonio also knows what it's like to work hard, having walked on to his college track-and-field team and earned a scholarship that demanded attention to both sport and study. But when he landed a job at Nickelodeon, he thought all of his dreams had come true, and he could finally relax.

"I was on TV every single day as the cohost of a live television show," he says. Millions of kids across the country tuned in to watch him interact with celebrity guests. It was everything he ever wanted.

Cue the autopilot.

Antonio went to work every day, doing all the things that had gotten him there, but none of the things necessary to keep him there. "They implored me to get better, to look at my reels, to look at the tape, just like I did as a college athlete, so I could become better at my craft," he remembers. "But I didn't. I was too distracted by fame, money, and autographs, and I was taking it all for granted."

One day, the producers informed him that the show was going in a different direction. Antonio knew this was entertainment business speak for: *You're fired*. He was out—in his mid-twenties and already a washed-up has-been.

He had escaped a life of financial and emotional insecurity and achieved everything he ever wanted. But he let it slip through his fingers. Now, with his family and friends back home still struggling, he had to deal with the guilt of making it big and then losing it all due to self-sabotage, laziness, and distraction.

That sent Antonio into a tailspin, culminating in his "cliché moment" of looking in the mirror and crying while cutting off his dreadlocks one by one. "I felt like my manual for life ran out of pages," he says.

Antonio had to make a decision: show up fully in his life and get things back in order, or just let life pass him by. He had glimpsed his potential and knew he was capable of more, but he didn't know how to get back on track to who he might become next. He was worried that the best thing to happen to him was already behind him.

But that wasn't the case. As Antonio was learning, we can start anew anytime we want. We just have to adopt a beginner's mindset.

For Antonio, that mindset led back to school: the graduate school at Columbia University, where his advisor was a Pulitzer Prize–winning author. "I used to hate turning in drafts of my thesis, because I knew they would come back covered in red ink," he explains.

Red ink meant lots of work to do.

One day, Antonio's advisor noticed his reluctance and asked, "Why are you turning this in late? What's your hesitation?" When Antonio explained about the red ink, the advisor said something he'll never forget: "Don't you know you pay for the red ink? That's where the magic is."

In an instant, Antonio finally saw what he had been missing: the "red ink" in his life was where improvement was possible, where his dreams could come true. So, he decided to be okay with going back to the start whenever he needed to improve or try again. He taught himself once more how to do the work, over and over, reinventing his dream and his purpose as many times as necessary.

Beware of Boredom

After running my last business to unexpected heights of success for ten years, I went into a pitch unprepared—totally, absolutely, positively, and in almost every way. I had been in executive search for fifteen years at that point, and it was the first time I had ever done anything like this—with a potential Big Deal Client, no less.

I wish I could say it was because I had been busy with other things, putting out fires at work and managing emergencies at home. But the truth of the matter is, I was just like Antonio. He got complacent. I got bored and overconfident. Just like him, I was on autopilot.

So dazzled was the Big Deal Client by my fancy dancing, contagious confidence, and fast-talking—most of which I was slinging straight out of my ass, thanks to years of experience and enough similar-sounding projects to bullshit my way through any discovery meeting—that he hired us on the spot. But walking out of his office, I knew immediately that I owed it to my team to move on.

The very next day, I started developing plans to sell my business to the women who had helped me build it.

Years later, I told a friend this story, complaining, "I just got sick of pitching."

He countered with a more accurate summation: "Laura, you just got sick of winning."

Things had gotten too easy. I was at the top of my game, and as a result, I'd started to do what top-rated business thinker Whitney Johnson describes, in her book *Disrupt Yourself*, as "unintentional self-sabotage." I was mailing it in, and eventually that was going to harm my company. Unless I made a different choice.

Had I not sold my business when I did, my staff and our clients would have felt the ripple effects of my growing ennui. I would have gotten impatient with them and burned through the best people. I would have become less contagiously confident with my clients, and less driven to help them see a future that could be theirs. I would have been less able to embolden them to make courageous hires who would help them change the world.

I would have ruined everything I had worked so hard to build, all because I didn't know how (or was too afraid) to move on and start over as a beginner on my next project.

The comfort of success—even when you may be crushing it—starts to feel a bit like boredom.

The repetition of the work—even the work you do so well—eventually blossoms into resentment about all the things that are no longer exciting and fun.

Performing the same roles and responsibilities over and over—even as this brings you greater and greater success—leaves you with nothing but emptiness and tedium.

If this sounds familiar, it's time to break the monotony and step into the unknown. Say goodbye to your past success, and prepare to jump out of that perfectly-functional-but-entirely-automated airplane. Increase the challenge. Build out a new offering. Or pack your parachute and move on.

Pack Your Parachute, and Everyone Else's, Too

Do you ever wonder what happens to people who go through a transformational reality-show makeover? After the show ends, the lights shut down, and the camera crew goes home, what comes next? The contestants have had a life-changing experience—lost a hundred pounds, experienced an emotional breakthrough, had their entire home redecorated, secured a record deal—but everyone around them has remained exactly the same.

That's the real show I want to watch. When someone goes through a massive change, can they sustain that change when they return to their former life? Can they remain that new, improved, "after" person once they're surrounded again by those who knew the "before" version?

Perhaps this has happened to you. If so, I'd hazard a guess that the outcome follows one of three paths: (a) your loved ones see your change, get inspired, and do the hard work to also change themselves; (b) they celebrate you momentarily and then go about their unchanged lives, leaving you alone on your island of transformation to wither, wallow, and eventually regress; or (c) they resent the hell out of you, and your very transformation becomes a source of friction and strife.

When something important is happening in your world, you can bet you're not the only one experiencing the upheaval that comes with a big change. So, as you peek out at your next Wonderhell, think about the people who might feel its impact: your boss, your employees, your colleagues, your friends, your family members.

What's the best way to approach this transition with them in mind? How will your changes affect them? How will you answer their questions about this change? What do you need from them as you move forward, and what do they need from you?

Whitney Johnson has a reminder for us: "When you are packing your own parachute, make sure that you are packing parachutes for everyone you want to bring with you, too."

On the day I decided to leave my executive search company and start over on a yet-to-be-determined path, I sat my business partner down and shared the news. After years of working together to get the business right—with me as the external face, bombastically telling the entire sector that executive recruitment could be done in a new and better way, and her as the internal one, tirelessly making sure that the quality of our new and better way fulfilled my lofty promises—we would soon go our separate ways.

We'd spent ten years innovating and growing, sometimes by 100 percent year over year. Now, though, I realized that for a while I'd been just mucking around with the business model and our service offerings. This met with some resistance from members of our team, which had started to bother me—and them. We already had a great model. It didn't need more tinkering. What the team needed was someone in love with the day-to-day work, not the under-the-hood innovation. My work there was basically done. The firm needed my business partner to lead it, not me.

This had become so obvious to me that I didn't understand how no one else could see it, too. I had to catch them up, lead them to the new starting line, and show them that the firm needed all of them more than it needed me. Rather than jump out of the plane quickly with the last parachute, I had to provide a soft landing for everyone else, too.

This was not an easy transition, and my final day wouldn't come until five years later. The process included mentors, lawyers, business consultants, and ultimately, an honest, face-to-face conversation over a bottle of scotch, about what my partner and I really wanted and how we could support each other to get there. Each of us had to look at the problem from the perspective of what the other needed, and what the firm needed.

I had to understand that my exit wasn't about me; it was really about them. My last day was my last day, but in many ways, it was their first day. And I had to understand how that might be terrifying.

Change is scary. Uncertainty is scary. Vulnerability is scary. Starting over is scary. This is true for everyone in the vicinity of your next Wonderhell. Expanding your focus to include not just your own parachute but also theirs will help ensure that everything works out fine, as it did for me. In fact, the firm thrived, and was recently ranked by *Forbes* among the Top 200 Executive

Search Firms in the United States across *all sectors* (not that I'm keeping score).

And it did so without me.

Take Your Ego Out of the Equation

If you've ever been to a parent-teacher conference, you probably know the discomfort of folding your too-long adult legs into a too-small child's chair. You probably also recall that awkward trickle of sweat that turns into a raging river as you listen to teachers telling you all the things your kids can't do.

It seems scary. *My kids are going to be failures! They're never going to move out of my house! They're going to live in the basement forever with their video games and their Hot Pockets!*

But actually, your kids are exactly where they need to be, and we can learn an important lesson from them. Each new school year, they repeat the process of adopting a beginner's mindset. They figure out algebra, and then it's time for geometry. They figure out geometry, and then it's time for trigonometry. They figure out trigonometry, and—hold the phone!—calculus is in the house. Over and over, year after year, our children learn that this beginner's mindset is not just okay. It's necessary. It's how they grow.

Some of the most successful people on our planet credit these moments in school for helping them do what had never been done before. Sergey Brin and Larry Page, co-founders of Google, are both children of academics, yet when asked about how this helped them become successful start-up entrepreneurs, they point instead to their Montessori School training, where there were no failures or dead ends—just new questions to ask. "Part of that training was being self-motivated," Page explains, "questioning what's going on in the world, doing things a little bit different."[1]

Yet somewhere along the line, we adults forget this lesson. We get hired to do something because, at one point, we demonstrated competence in that thing. We get paid, praised, and even promoted for it. Then time passes,

---

1 Sophie Fleetwood, "The Montessori Method: The 5 Principles," *Mindsplain*, 2021.

and we become so afraid that if we try something else, we might fail. We think our ego can't survive that—and maybe our career can't either. So we stick to the same path even as we are nervously eyeing our next Wonderhell.

I wrote in *Limitless* about how failure is not finale, it's fulcrum. And I believe it is . . . for most of us.

Once, while giving a keynote in Austin, Texas, I shouted from the stage, "Failure's not finale. It's fulcrum!" And then I looked down to see Commander Tim Kopra of NASA sitting in the front row. As an astronaut, Kopra went on three separate spacewalks while flying missions aboard the International Space Station. So I hastened to add, "Except for you, sir!" For an astronaut on a spacewalk, failure would most definitely be finale.

But for the rest of us, failure isn't the end of the road—not as long as there is blood in our veins and oxygen in our lungs—unless we let it be. Failure is just the red ink. It's where we iterate and innovate and learn and grow and get better.

So we have to expect failure, and even welcome it, each and every time we go back to the beginning and start on our next Wonderhell. This means taking our ego out of the equation and allowing ourselves room to fail spectacularly. Because starting over again from scratch is often the only way forward.

Starting from Scratch

Whitney Johnson doesn't just want you to start over. She's done it herself, too.

A music major in college, Whitney went to Wall Street and became a top-ranked analyst in multiple categories. She was good at the work and was at the top of her game.

But she had begun to learn about a globally respected thinker at Harvard Business School, Clayton Christensen. As she studied Christensen's work, she had an aha moment. His signature idea of disruption wasn't just about products and services, but also about people. Whitney had been successful as a financial analyst, but she'd reached the high point of what she was inspired to do in that role. When she told her boss that she had cold-called Christensen and was planning to join him in academia, her boss warned that she was making a huge mistake.

"When you make a move and everybody thinks you've lost your mind, it's because there's a calculus that not everyone can see," she says. You were hired to do a functional job that puts money in your bank account and food on your table, but the equation also includes an emotional element to the job: *Am I enjoying this? Do I feel satisfied? Do I feel fulfilled? Am I learning and growing and developing?* Even when the functional piece is still happening, the emotional cost sometimes becomes too high to stay.

Investing alongside Christensen at Harvard was exciting, interesting, and ever-changing, and that inspired Whitney for a while. But then, after watching Clayton lecture about the work to thousands of people all over the world, she once again wanted something more.

"He's kind of a rock star, right?" one of Whitney's colleagues remarked. "People listen to what he has to say!"

And a voice inside of Whitney whispered, *Yes. I want that, too.* That's how she came to write her first book, give her first speeches, and become one of the top business thinkers in the world.

Leaving Wall Street was a leap. Pushing herself out of her comfort zone, from ivory tower research to the public sphere, was another. Each time, she had to get comfortable restarting as a beginner, knowing that she was not going to get it right every step of the way. Starting again from scratch is disruptive. It is messy. And sometimes, it is the road to brilliance.

Disruptive ideas and products spread through a culture like an S curve—a graphic illustration depicted half a century ago by E. M. Rogers (who also introduced us to the term *early adopter*). These ideas start small, unheard of and unknown, and then they catch fire, swooping upward and finally becoming part of the zeitgeist. In her books and presentations, Whitney decided to take this S curve and apply it to people's lives. We start not knowing anything, failing fast and failing often. But then we hit a magic moment when everything clicks, and finally that knowledge and understanding are just part of who we are.

Remember Antonio's story, though? Remember mine? Hang out at this sweet spot too long, and the incline flattens. We stop growing. We stop learning. We get bored. That's when we have to leap to a new S curve, where we start the whole process again.

I don't want you to think this is easy, though. Even Whitney had trouble starting from scratch. She admits to being so overwhelmed at first, so terrified, so cowed by the desire to shift to her next Wonderhell that she couldn't look directly at it. "Maybe if I don't look at the mountain," she told herself, "I won't have to face the climb."

So, for a while, she sat at the flat end of her S curve and pretended the mountain didn't even exist. She stayed put. She kept doing the same work she'd been doing.

Yet although she wasn't consciously moving forward, her subconscious had already made the decision. She'd crossed the Rubicon, even if just mentally. When it came time to make the big leap into her next Wonderhell, she found that she'd been gathering everything she needed the whole time.

ARE YOU READY FOR THIS RIDE?

Staying too long at the pinnacle carries a unique danger: the risk of going on autopilot, getting complacent, or unwittingly sabotaging everything you've worked for up until now. Yet it is scary to leave the security of success, especially when it means you'll be starting from the bottom.

Knowing when it is time to start over on the Loop-de-Loop—either with a clean slate or just by introducing more complex challenges around the edges—is key to thriving throughout each successive Wonderhell. You can restart on your own terms, or you can wait around for it to happen without your consent. Either way, get comfortable with putting yourself in charge of whether that restart button sparks an implosion or an explosion.

As you determine whether it is time to loop back to a new start, consider the following questions:

- What part of your work is still exciting, and what part has produced emotions like boredom or resentment?
- Who do you need to support you in the leap to your next adventure, and how can you ensure that they are ready for that transition, too?
- Which failures would be catastrophic, and which can you withstand—even learn from—as part of the process?

THE SOUVENIR SHOP

LIVING IN WONDERHELL

I am quite a slow runner. In fact, to even call it running is somewhat insulting to runners. I ran the first mile—of my life—a few weeks before I turned thirty-nine. It took me six weeks to get to the point of not needing to stop again and again to catch my breath (and maybe puke). But once I got there, I couldn't help but think, *You know, if I string three of those together, I could run a 5K.*

A few months later, as I crossed the finish line of that 5K, I thought, *You know, if I string two of those together, I could run a 10K.*

You see where this is going, right? Friends, I live in Boston.

Fast-forward one year. I was at the halfway point of my first Boston Marathon, a bib I earned by raising money for a charity that was close to my heart. It was unseasonably hot, a 92-degree day whose forecast pressured race organizers to offer deferrals to race entrants concerned about the risk of death. I stopped to greet a friend on the course—when you are as slow as me, and it's as hot as that, you're not too concerned about breaking land-speed records—and he exclaimed, "Wesley Korir just finished the race in two hours and twelve minutes!"[1]

It had taken me two and a half hours to even get halfway, and Wesley was already done. Earlier on the course, my husband had stuffed bags of ice into my sports bra. A woman cheering from the sidewalk a mile or two later pointed to them and yelled, "What a great idea!"

---

1 For context, this is a mere ten minutes slower than the course record set just one year earlier, in perfect cool and dry conditions, by Geoffrey Mutai.

And I looked down, dumbfounded, and couldn't even remember how they got there. At that point, even the details of my own name were beginning to get a little fuzzy.

I was tired, I was hurting, and things were beginning to chafe in all the wrong places. The longest effort in marathon training is a twenty-mile run; I wasn't even there yet. But I was still so young and naïve at that point in the race. I was still certain that I was going to finish.

About an hour and a half of run-slogging later, I found myself having finally crested the aptly named Heartbreak Hill—a series of rolling hills between miles 17 and 21 that hit the runner right at the point of intolerance. I had reached mile 20.

I was no longer young and naïve. I was, at best, old and wizened.

And I found myself thinking, *I wonder what happens now?*

My shoes were *squish-squish-squishing* on the melting black asphalt. The sun was beating down on my scalp, frying my brain like eggs. The sports bra ice Ziplocs had long since transitioned to warm, sloshing soup. I was deep into my pain cave.

As I continued to run-slog past the many other dehydrated runners scattered throughout the first-aid tents all around me, I began to hallucinate. A voice inside me screamed, *Oh my god, what are you doing? This was the dumbest thing you've ever done in your life! All these people are watching you. All these people are relying on you. All these people supported you. You're going to fail. You're going to die.*

I was in hell.

But another voice—a softer, sneakier one—whispered, *You can do this. You are going to finish. Someone is going to put a medal around your neck and a silver mylar blanket around your body, and you will be a freaking superhero. Run, walk, crawl across that finish line—it doesn't matter. You are going to be a marathoner for the rest of your life.*

I was in hell, but I was also in wonder.

In your moments of Wonderhell, only one of those voices gets to win. And the only person who gets to decide which one wins is you.

You, and only you, get to decide if you will remain in hell, or if you will live into the wonder.

At that moment, struggling along in record-setting heat toward my five-plus-hour projected finish, I realized that Wesley Korir probably had these same thoughts when he went deep into his pain cave, too. I was running as hard and fast as I could. But Wesley had pushed his own winning pace in the same record-setting heat, running as hard and fast as he could, too.

It was challenging for me, with my training, my level of experience, my amount of fitness, and my track record of (modest) success, to reach my desired goal. But it was also challenging for him to accomplish his goal, even with all his training, experience, fitness, and (enviable) success.

Wesley Korir finished that race first, but we'd both danced with those demons that reside at the darkest depths of our personal pain caves, screaming at us to slow down, to give in, to stop. While those caves might look different for each of us, the exquisite, local, personal pain of maximum effort feels exactly the same.

This is your Wonderhell. It's where you figure out what more you are made of, what more you can do, and what more you can be.

Because Wonderhell isn't your breakdown. It's your breakthrough.

Wonderhell invites you to dive into that discomfort.

Wonderhell urges you to expand your boundaries.

Wonderhell introduces you to your true promise.

Wonderhell asks, *Are you going to let this moment pass you by? Or are you going to live into your budding potential and power?*

Well, are you?

It's time to find out.

OVERFLOW PARKING

ACKNOWLEDGMENTS

In early 2021, I was diagnosed with an incredibly rare autoimmune disorder that affects eight hundred people in the entire United States. Truth be told, I didn't know if I would see 2022. Writing the first version of this book—85,000 of the worst words you'd ever read—allowed me to cling, through ten months of chemotherapy infusions, to my identity as a thinker and a writer, even when my brain and my hands (and every other body part) didn't agree.

I put it down when I could no longer move it forward, finally picking up the bloated, nonsensical manuscript a full year later and taking a mental machete to the shit sandwich that lay before me. The shorter, tighter, and (I hope) better version you have in your hands or in your ears is thanks to a support system that I don't deserve and yet count among my blessings on a daily basis.

Clay Hebert was the first to recognize that Wonderhell was a good idea, reading that very first exhausted social media rant where I flippantly threw out the concept (thinking nothing of it in a sea of my other similar screeds), commenting, "Wonderhell is a brilliant word." Michael Barber noted that the URL of Wonderhell.com was available, and why not pick it up for $0.99? Rohit Bhargava, my publisher, piled on as well, noting that Wonderhell would make an excellent name for my next book. I could not get the idea out of my mind. Together, these seeds germinated in my brain in ways I could not unsee.

Rahaf Harfoush was my second brain throughout most of these past two years, seeing order in my chaos, and wrapping sense and theme around my verbal vomit during weekly calls when I couldn't keep track of my own thoughts. Clay Hebert and David Burkus were murder board and support system all wrapped into one. Bret Simmons and his team at TEDx-Reno punched my idea around with me until I could talk about it in a tight twelve minutes. Liane Davey sent me articles that underscored random ideas I'd mentioned in our chats. Mitch Joel checked in on me daily, with a perfectly ironed-out closetful of bitching, gossiping, humor, and wisdom. Jackie Summers refused to let me believe my own excuses. Carey Lohrenz makes everything and everyone in her path better, including me. Amy Dorta McIlwaine has the patience of an editing angel. Tiffani Bova pinged me if I went silent for too long and reminded me how big my ideas could be. Tasha Eurich took her own PhD machete in the form of a red pen to the penultimate, printed version of this book, not letting me get away with any psychobabble or motivational bullshit that wasn't backed up by good old honest research. My goodness, you are a brilliant bunch.

And Drs. Herschenfeld and Sobel, maybe this is weird to say, but this book wouldn't be here without you—and maybe neither would I. So, I tip my hat to your curiosity, persistence, and medical genius.

As I said in *Limitless*, there is family, and there is framily. I am lucky to have both. To my parents, my sister, my cousin, and my in-laws, your patience as I circled around and around new ideas did not go unnoticed, nor did your patience to let me do this while I should have been doing nothing at all. I heard your lectures, and I appreciate that you looked the other way as I ignored them entirely. To Ilona Goldfarb and Jameila Haddawi, thank you for letting me talk your ear off about random emotions and even more random symptoms. And to Beth Hoffman, thank you (I think!) for all the miles we ran. Your steady and sturdy friendships mean more to me than you could ever comprehend.

To those who joined my early reader squad—Jonathan Acox, Julie Balasalle, Doug Brown, Katie Bulota, Elayne Burke, Robert Calacino, Celine Coggins, Lisa D'Amore, Dayna Del Val, Sylvia Farbstein, Casey Fogle, Nicole Gann, Michelle Hynes, Javier La Fianza, Clare Lawrence, Frances Moseley, Sam Ruhmkorff, Joe Schoolcraft, Darryl Seaton, John Tigh, Rob Toller—

all I can say is "Wow!" This book is vastly improved because of your energy, effort, and edits.

To Juniper, who spent most of the writing of this book with one paw wrapped around me, I know I owe you a coauthor credit, but that's not how publishing works. Sorry. I'll throw an extra bone in your dinner tonight.

To my children, Benjamin and Tobias, I'll let you in on a little secret. When I was at my lowest, trying to be the person you saw when you looked at me was what kept me going. It's what has shaped me into who I continue to become—not just this past year, but in all the years prior and all the years to come. Maybe I'm raising you, but you are also raising me, too.

To my husband, Jonathan, I can think of no one I'd rather ride with through the Tunnel of Love, and every other ride in every other park. Saying yes to that Thursday night date, even though it broke *The Rules*, was the only time I ever didn't listen to advice in a book—and it was the best decision I ever made. Where you are, my heart will always be.

Finally, to all those who lent me their stories, thank you for allowing me to root around in your worst days so we can make sense of your best days. I am forever in your debt.

And to you, the reader, I am nothing without the faith and trust that you put in me each time you read my words. You picked up this book because you suspected that you were meant for more. I know it's true, and I hope you now know it, too.

OVERFLOW PARKING

Resources

★

If you enjoyed Wonderhell, please take a moment to leave a review on Amazon.com. That helps other readers just like you find this book.

To continue the conversation, visit http://www.wonderhell.com. There you can download some free goodies (including a book group guide) to help you through your next Wonderhell. You'll also find all sorts of other things, like our newsletter, courses, and other fun stuff.

Laura Gassner Otting is available to speak to your organization, community, or event. More details at http://www.LauraGassnerOtting.com.